GROWING UP SANDY

Memories of a Baby Boomer

BY

SANDY FIELDEN CUNNINGHAM

Growing Up Sandy

ISBN: 9781979495912

Printed in the USA by

Dedication

I want to dedicate this book to:

My parents – Paul and Marjene Fielden whose love inspired me to always be the best I could be. My sister – Susan Kay Fielden Prew whose love and companionship have always inspired me to be better.

My husband – Dale L. Cunningham whose love has sustained me for 59 years and who has inspired me to keep going, never to quit.

To my three children – Kenny, Jason and Julie – the three miracles in my life.

Special Thank You to:

Bonnie Howitz, my lifelong friend

And

Carol Ihrig, Girl Scout friend and mentor,

For their help in editing this book.

Table of Contents

Introduction

I grew up in a small Midwestern town, Plymouth, Michigan. Plymouth is located about thirty-two miles outside of Detroit. When I was growing up in the 1950s and 1960s, Detroit was the great Motor City – home to the Ford Motor Company, General Motors, Chrysler, and American Motors. Plymouth, though, was a rural town of about 8,000 people. There was a Main Street, a park in the middle of downtown – Kellogg Park – Church Street with the Methodist and Presbyterian Churches, and the high school and there was Lower Town where you could find the train station, the First Baptist Church, and two small grocery stores – Bill's Market and the Lidgard Market. It was a beautiful, quiet little town surrounded by farms.

My family was small, just Momma, Daddy, Grandma Lidgard and me, Sandy, until I was ten years old and my sister Susan arrived. Daddy was a meat-cutter, store owner, and businessman. Momma helped Daddy in his store as his cashier. And Grandma stayed home and took care of me. And that is where my story begins.

Grandma would tell me stories about covered wagons, soddy huts, gypsies, and life on the prairie. In that way, she introduced me to history and to Caroline, Nathan, Nelson, and others in her family. But I was too young to ask her questions about what she did as a child, something I greatly regret. I did ask my parents and I have some really good material to share along the way.

This is my story of growing up in the 1950s and 1960s. My memories of the friends I met along the way, the games we played, our holiday traditions, playing in the band, meeting my some-day husband. It's the story of some of the people who helped me to grow – Girl Scout leaders, teachers, my parents and my friends. Most of all, it's the story of growing up in a loving and supportive family who gave me the love and support I needed to become Sandy.

It is written for my children and grand-children and those yet to come. It is written so that they will know me and the circumstances of my time. The stories and memories here will take you from the early days of my life through the day I became the wife of my lifetime partner, Dale Cunningham. There will be more books and memories to follow as time passes, but for now, I hope you will enjoy "Growing Up Sandy" and, perhaps, find yourself in these pages, too.

Two Hearts Filled with Love

As told by Paul and Marjene Fielden

He left the farm in Hines Creek outside Knoxville, Tennessee, in the fall of 1938. His future was in Michigan, where he thought there would be work. William Paul Fielden (Paul) was twenty-one years old and he hoped for a better life than the impoverished farm life he was leaving behind.

Working his way north, he stopped first in Indiana to harvest tomatoes. Found his way next to Wixom, Michigan, located in the southeast corner of the state. He found work first harvesting potatoes on the Manning farm. Paul helped grade the potatoes as well and then truck them into Detroit to the farmer's market. The Mannings liked this soft spoken young man and asked him to stay on and help them farm after the harvest. By 1940, he had learned his way

around southeastern Michigan well enough to move on once again. This time, he went to work for Bob and Clarence Lidgard in Plymouth, Michigan – a small town about thirty-two miles outside of Detroit. They owned a small, family run market – Lidgard's Grocery. Here he would find his future, as a grocer and a meat cutter, under their tutelage and friendship. And here, he would find his life partner.

1

It was here in the spring of 1940 that Bob's wife Lucille took it upon herself to introduce her young sister-in-law, nineteen-year-old Marjene, to the soft-spoken Paul Fielden. She convinced Bob that Marjene needed to work at the store. Marjene became the cashier and helped to stock the store. At five feet tall, she frequently needed help putting stock on the upper shelves. She would stand on a ladder and Paul would hand the goods up to her. There was one incident where she dropped a can on his foot! Her brothers also concocted a long stick with a hook on one end so that she could reach and pull things down from those upper shelves.

By the summer of 1940, Paul and Marjene were dating. They would go to Detroit Tiger baseball games in Detroit or to the movies. Sometimes they would double date with their friends Frank Columbo and Ruth Levenworth, her friends from high school. By Christmas, they knew they were in love and began talking about marriage. His gift to her that Christmas was a golden locket with his picture on one side.

Money was a problem, though, and they felt they weren't financially in a position to get married. Paul was making $22.00 a week at the store and Marjene was making $10.00 a week. His room and board was $4.00 a week and she helped him out by doing his laundry. So, to make their dreams come true, Paul enlisted in the Army on March 28, 1941. The plan was for him to serve a one year hitch while they saved all their money and then to marry when his hitch (one year of Army enlistment) was over. Little did they know what was to come on December 7, 1941.

They were hundreds of miles away from each other on that fateful December day that would change their plans and their lives. Marjene was in Northville, Michigan. She and her friends had gone to church that morning and then left to see a movie before the announcement came over the radio about the bombing of Pearl Harbor. They were at the movie when the announcement came. Meanwhile, Paul was lying on his bunk in San Luis Obispo, California, relaxing after a long week of maneuvers. As an engineer unit, their assignment was building and assembling pontoon bridges for military equipment to use where there were no roads. Paul had heard rumors that something BIG was happening that day, but until formation was called at 3:00 PM, he did not know what was truly happening. Within hours of the announcement, his unit pulled out of San Luis Obispo and headed for the Mexican border, where they would stand guard against attack from foreign enemies.

World War II was now exploding in the south Pacific. His unit, the 115th Combat engineers, part of the 40th Infantry, was moved to Ft. Lewis, Washington, in April of 1942. From here, they were scheduled to ship out to an unknown assignment in the Pacific basin. With their future now in jeopardy, Paul and Marjene decided to get married. A short time of happiness for them was better than no happiness at all.

In June of 1942, Marjene purchased train tickets and began her journey to Olympia, Washington. The train trip was three long, boring days. She was one month short of her twenty-first birthday and traveling alone on the train. An older woman befriended her and kept her company part of the way. Sandwiches and "pop" were brought around the crowded cars to help feed those traveling to meet loved ones and those traveling to new duty stations. Once the train crossed the Rocky Mountains, black out curtains were placed on the windows to keep the train from being seen from the sky by enemy aircraft from as it moved west.

Paul was unable to meet the train when it arrived, so Marjene took a taxi to the hotel. The attendant at the hotel made a call to Paul's unit and left a message that she had arrived safely. Early the next morning, June 20, 1942, Paul arrived at the hotel, and they left to get their marriage license. His company commander had tied two passes together so that Paul was off from Saturday morning through Monday.

Their plans to get a license in the morning and be married in the afternoon were thwarted when they arrived at the courthouse. The line was long and, when they finally reached the window, they were told that the judge would be leaving for the weekend in a few minutes. They made their decision quickly, and there, in an empty courthouse, with a janitor and a clerk as witnesses, Paul and Marjene were married – no ring, no flowers, no friends. What they did have was two hearts filled with love and a dream for the future.

They left the courthouse and returned to the hotel. Marjene changed into the dress she had selected for her marriage – a navy blue slip dress with an over "coat" of navy blue with white polka dots. (This color combination would become a favorite for her in the years to come.) While she changed, Paul returned to the barracks where he put on his dress uniform, picked up the wedding ring and stopped by the florist for the corsage of red roses he had selected for his bride. Tom Gasparovich, his best friend in the unit, joined them at the hotel, where they enjoyed a wedding lunch and then left to see a movie, "Anchors Aweigh," starring Frank Sinatra and Gene Kelly. After the movie, they went to the park to gaze at Mount Olympia.

Marjene stayed in Olympia for nine days before she boarded the train to return to Michigan. They had been able to spend their evenings together. He was able to accompany her as far as the rain station before they said their good-byes. It would be another three years before they would see each other again, and those years would be perilous ones.

On June 20, 1992, Paul and Marjene celebrated their 50th anniversary by repeating their marriage vows in church with their two daughters, six of their grandchildren, and other family and friends attending. They had shared many wonderful years together since Marjene's cross country wedding trip. On this day, she once again wore navy blue and white with a corsage of red roses. The biggest surprise of the day was the arrival of their best man, Tom Gasparovich, who stopped by to help celebrate their special day. Their marriage lasted for fifty-six years and left a strong legacy of love and partnership for their family.

Along Came Sandy

World War II was over, but ships were still arriving in New York, San Francisco and Los Angeles, bringing servicemen home to the United States. Daddy had served in the South Pacific and had returned in early 1945. Momma had joined him in Miami Beach where he was stationed at one of the Army's Rest and Recreation Hotels. They returned at the end of the war, in August of 1945, to Michigan to start their lives together.

Now, on this cold, grey February day, February 8, 1946 to be sure, I made my appearance in their lives. They gave me the name Sandra Lenore, and I would forever be called Sandy. I would also be part of a new generation, born following the war, we would be known as "Baby Boomers", and as one of the largest generations ever born, we would make our presence known all through our lives.

We went home to a small house in Northville, Michigan that we shared with Grandma Lidgard. No one knew then that our house would one day become a historic house because of its strange architecture – it was octagonal. Quite naturally, I don't remember living there but my parents had tales to tell. For one thing, I was a fussy baby and I would cry very loudly during the night. My parents' solution to that problem was to put me in the closet and shut the door! The "closet" was actually a very small room off their bedroom. We did not live there very long. When I was three months

old, we moved to a small, one-bedroom house at 744 South Harvey, in Plymouth, Michigan.

These first few years of my life are more feelings and memories from stories my parents told and pictures that they took. My baby book is filled with all my "firsts" and with pictures of those first exploits – sitting, walking, holding my teddy bear. I think I must have known that I was loved by the people in my world – Momma, Daddy, Grandma Lidgard and our neighbors, the Zimmerman's.

When I was two years old, I became an adventurer. There was the time I woke up before my parents and went for a walk out to the garage! Our neighbor, Mr. Zimmerman, caught me and delivered me back to my parents. Another time, I decided to go see the Zimmerman's while I was supposed to be taking a nap. After that excursion, my parents decided to build a pen in the back yard where I could play safely and not go exploring. Only one thing was left for me – climbing the cherry tree that they included in my pen. One day my mom came out the back door with a load of laundry to hang on the clothesline. She found me hanging in the tree, caught by my belt loop! I couldn't get down and she couldn't reach me! Once again, she called on the neighbors to get me out of the tree. Yes, I kept my parents busy!

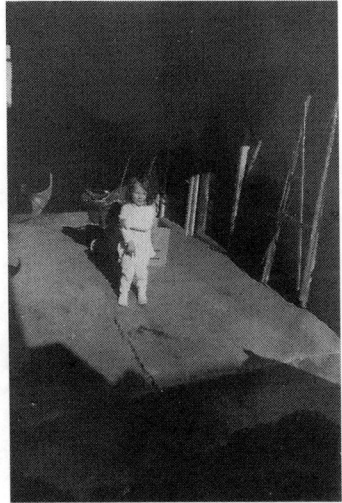

By the time I was three years old, I had outgrown my backyard pen. Now, I wandered one block farther, and found my first playmate, Ellen Kay. Ellen Kay's family had come from Syria to the United States. She lived in a two-story house with her parents, two brothers, her grandmother and an uncle. Her father and uncle owned a grocery store and in years to come, would be close friends with my parents.

Ellen and I became fast friends and remained so through high school. She and I learned to climb trees, play cowboys and Indians and get into the kinds of trouble little girls get into.

One of our biggest crimes took place in her parent's garage. Her

family had painted the interior of their house and there were lots of pails of "just a little bit" of paint in them. Well, they didn't paint their garage so Ellen and I took it upon ourselves to use up the different colors of paint and paint the garage.

Her dad was not happy at all! We were both punished for that prank and her father said he was never going to let us forget. Well, almost! On the night we graduated from high school, Mr. Elias gave us our graduation gift – he finally had the garage painted one color!!

Mrs. Zimmerman, her grandson Larry and I all shared the same birthday, well almost. Her birthday was February 2 and mine was the 8th and Larry's somewhere in between. We all celebrated together until I was well into high school. She would always make a meal for us, usually fried chicken or spaghetti, and a wonderful cake. Ummmm!! She always made wonderful goodies but her cakes and cookies were the best.

We moved away from South Harvey when I was six years old. But I have many wonderful, warm memories of my first friend and the wonderful people who surrounded me and kept me safe those first few years.

The Man Behind the Counter

Today when we go grocery shopping in our brightly lit superstores, we go to the meat department and choose our steaks, chicken or hamburger from an open counter. The meats are prepackaged into different cuts and laid out neatly in the counter.

This was not so in the past – the 1940s and 1950s. Back then, meat counters were found at the back of the store, usually in the back right corner. The counters were shiny bright enamel, and the meat was enclosed behind glass on the customer side and black sliding doors on the backside. The fresh cuts of meat were displayed on steel trays. And there, behind the counter, was the man who had cut all that meat – The Man Behind the Counter.

The man behind the meat counter for me was my dad, William Paul Fielden, popularly called Paul by his friends and family, and Bill by his associates in the business. He had learned his trade from my mother's brothers, Bob and Clarence Lidgard, before World War II in their small grocery store in Plymouth, Michigan. After the war, he had worked at Sears department store in the tire department; finding it unsatisfactory, he soon found himself behind the meat counter once again.

As a child growing up, I found his world behind the counter exciting and mysterious. There were all kinds of *strange and mysterious machines and tools back there!* There was always a large table called a *butcher block*. It was a large, heavy table that looked like it was made out of squares of wood. This was where Daddy cut the meat into steaks, roasts, chops and so on from the larger sides of beef or pork. Chickens were also chopped up into chicken breasts, legs, and thighs. The tools he used were sharp meat cleavers of all different lengths that he kept hanging on the side of the block. I can still see him standing beside the block sharpening the knives on the long pointed steel, whisking the knives up and down, up and down, ever so quickly to sharpen the blades.

Then there was his large saw. The saw was used to cut the sides of beef down into pieces that were easier to handle and to cut through the bones. Here he cut up sides of ribs and pork chops. ZZZZZZew would go the saw as it went through the bones. Then back to the butcher block to scrape away the splattered fat and bone from the meat.

There was his big walk-in meat cooler where I could find all kinds of adventures and *"imagine sinister tales."* The handle itself was scary enough! It was a plunger handle, meaning you pushed against it to open the door. It was the same from the inside of the cooler but always seemed heavier from the inside, and I was **always** afraid of getting locked inside. Because, inside the cooler, were these huge hooks with sides of meat hanging from them. I could always imagine where the meat came from, and then I could imagine hanging there myself! **Oh, no!**

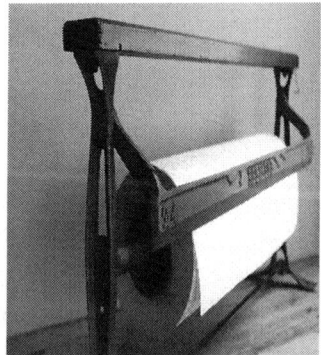

Dad always had sawdust spread on the floor behind the counter and large barrels of the fresh sawdust ready to spread. Every night after closing, he would sweep up the old sawdust and spread the fresh, ready for tomorrow's business. The sawdust was used because it helped soak up the blood and debris from the meat, making it easier to clean the floors. Daddy always had a second pair of shoes to wear home at night so he wouldn't bring any old sawdust back to the house.

Behind the counter itself was another whole world. Daddy would stand behind the counter and wait on his customers. He referred to it as "serving" his customers. Here the customer would ask for a specific piece of meat from the counter or make their own request, "I'd like four steaks and make them about so thick," as they raised their hands with fingers splayed apart to indicate the thickness. Or maybe they wanted "that" roast but, "could you please cut off the fat." Then there were the lunch meat requests, always indicating their preference for thin or thicker slices. Lunch meat was always cut from the roll; it did not come prepackaged in neat little boxes. Daddy would meet their needs then pull the thick brown butcher paper from the big roll, pulling it through the cutter. He'd lay it on the wrapping shelf behind the counter, folding the paper this way and that just so, then taping it shut. He'd pull the grease pencil from his pocket and mark the price on the paper wrapper.

The slicer he used to cut the lunch meat was actually one of the most dangerous tools he used. He would hold the meat with one hand as he slid it through the slicing blade.

Things weren't so bad when the piece of lunch meat was six inches long; but when you got closer to the end, your fingers were really close to the blade. I remember the night he brought his assistant Jim home with him after a stint at the emergency room. Jim had cut the end of his finger off in the slicer!

There was always a place for Sandy behind the counter. He usually let me have the run of the place as long as I stayed out of his way and didn't interfere with the customers. My imagination could run wild behind the counter, and I made up all kinds of horror fantasies in his butcher world. Of course, when it was really busy, I had to be curtailed, so he always kept a box of crayons in his desk so I could draw pictures on the butcher paper he'd tear off for that purpose, a skill I used many times as a Girl Scout leader and Program Director in the years to come.

Daddy was a meat cutter most of his life. He would try other things along the way but would always go back to cutting meat, either in his own store or for other friends. The first place he worked was at Mason's Market in Farmington, Michigan. He followed that by renting the meat department at Inkster market in Inkster, Michigan. From there, he owned the Paul Mar Market in Plymouth for many years. He then found a larger store in South Lyon, Michigan, and bought what he named The Grandway Market. Along the way, he worked for his friend Lon Dickerson at Dickerson's Market in Plymouth or the Elias Brothers' Market in Livonia. In the end, he went to work at Kroger in their meat department as a master meat cutter. He retired from Kroger in 1982. When he owned his own business, my mother would work by his side. They were both highly respected and loved by their steady customers.

Probably my biggest and best memory of my dad behind the counter was just seeing him – fresh as he started out each day. He'd be dressed in his bright white, freshly starched apron, with a white shirt and tie. There was always a bright smile and that wonderful soft southern accent. He was truly **The Man Behind the Counter.**

Mom and Dad behind the meat counter

Endearing Qualities

Paul Fielden, my daddy, was a quiet, gentle man with many hidden traits only we, his family, got to see and enjoy. Born and raised in the soft rolling hills and valleys of the Great Smoky Mountains, he spoke with a hint of his southern upbringing all of his life. When it came to his family, be it brothers, sisters, daughters, or wife, he was a strong defender with a heart as soft as his voice.

One of his most endearing qualities could be found in his way of speaking. His tongue had a funny way of curling up when he wanted to say certain things. One of our favorites was when he thought something was "weeried" – pronounced we-ear-ied. Like when the sky turned a "weeried" shade of green or a person in his store acted "weeried." You know – weird! And he was really careful of his cars – he always had the "ool" changed on a regular basis. But, the favorite of his grandchildren was when he would catch them jumping on the furniture and he would yell, "STOP! You're going to "rrun" – pronounced rune – the furniture!"

Not only did Daddy have a language of his own, he also had a way of "fixing" things like no one else! He was not known for his ability as a fix-it man or mechanic, but he was always willing to give it a try. Christmas trees were very low on his list – I think he actually hated them. In Michigan, we always had a fresh cut tree. We would eagerly go out and pick a tree from the tree lot and bring it home. That's when the fun always started. Daddy would get the stand out and place the tree in it and, inevitably, the trunk wasn't straight or the tree leaned too far one way or another. This led to cutting the trunk to make it right. I can remember going to get a second tree because the first one got too short or had too many branches cut off! Then there was the year the tree was tied to the wall behind it and, of course, there was the year he anchored the tree to the ceiling to keep it straight!

Another of his favorite inventions as a fix-it man was the television antenna. Before cable TV, we all had antennas anchored to the roof so we could receive a TV signal and our programs. Well, Daddy always had to fiddle with the antenna to get it "just right." His most famous antenna was in our house on North Harvey street during the 1960s and 1970s. This antenna was actually in his attic and by the time he got it "just right," it was held in place with clip clothespins, hangers, and aluminum foil, and it took over the attic!

There came a time when my sister Susie needed a vacuum cleaner. Daddy loaned his old vacuum cleaner for her to use. She realized it needed a new bag before she could use it. When she took the old bag out, she discovered another of our dad's "fixes." The old bag had obviously been emptied before and torn in the process. Rather than getting a new bag, he had stapled all the sides of the bag together and made it work! Yes, Daddy believed you could "fix" anything with hangers, staples, clothespins, and duct tape.

The most endearing of his charms was the way he treated our mother, Marjene. He worshipped the ground she walked on and would do anything for her. However, he didn't always do her bidding quietly. Frequently, he was asked to do something while he was reading "his" newspaper. He would rattle the newspaper loudly and make a big show out of putting it down and as he walked away, you could hear him say," Damn it, Marjene!" One of our favorites occurred when they did the dishes together which happened more often in retirement. Mom would wash the dishes and Daddy would dry them, and Momma would always get ahead of him by going too fast. "Damn it, Marjene!" would come clearly echoing out of the kitchen to the

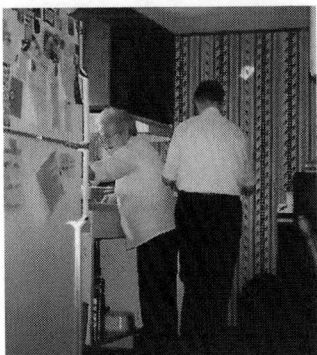

extent that one of his granddaughters thought "Damn it, Marjene!" was her grandma's name!

He had a special song that he sang to Susie and me and to our children. We heard it when we needed cheering up, it was our "lullaby," and it was our song of celebration. When I was homesick and living in Germany, he sang it to me on a tape and sent it to me. When Susie got home from the airport with her oldest daughter, Jenny – adopted from Columbia – Susie placed her in Daddy's arms and he began to sing. Jenny, three months old, snuggled right into his arms and fell asleep. The song he sang was "Little Brown Jug," and the very last line went, "Little Brown Jug, don't I love thee!" and we always knew that he did – love us.

Lady in Red

I think I knew from the moment I first opened my eyes on this great big world that the safest and most wonderful place to be was by my mother's side. She was never my "mother," she was always my "momma." There is only one word that I have ever found that totally describes Momma, *Lady*.

Marjene Lidgard Fielden was the youngest of eight children. She had five older brothers and two older sisters. Her early life was not an easy one. She had lived through the Great Depression as a young child and teenager and then began her married life on June 20, 1942, by sending my dad, Paul, to the South Pacific for three years in World War II. Momma had worked hard as a child and a young adult – helping my grandparents in their store and working as a nurse's aide during the war. Being the youngest in her family, she was used to hand-me-down clothes and toys. But somehow, none of that seemed to have daunted her. Momma always seemed to take things in stride with a smile on her face.

When I was just a *little* girl, up to the age of ten, I was an only child and the center of my parents' world. My grandfather had passed away two months before I was born, so my Grandma Lidgard was part of our family, too. Those days were totally idyllic! My mother, Auntie Arvella, her older sister by twenty years, and my grandma would get together and DO all kinds of wonderful things. During the winter, they would get together and quilt in our living room. For a whole week, the quilting frame would be up and they would laugh and tell stories as their fingers put the fine stitches into the quilt. I would sit under the quilt and listen to their laughter and their stories.

The summer was canning time, and again they would be together, either at our house or my aunt's larger house. They would scald the tomatoes and pour them into the canning jars, steaming them to seal the freshness inside. Then came the pickles – the pungent smell of vinegar filled the air as they poured the different spice mixtures into the vinegar and cucumbers – sweet pickles, bread and butter pickles, and dills. I can still hear their laughter echoing through the air. Now and then, one of them would burst into song, "Oh! Solo Mio!" Of course, they couldn't leave out all the wonderful fruits! Heavens NO! We had peach jam, canned peaches, cherry jam, and canned pears. Oh, the harvest was marvelous and ever so yummy!!

Then came late fall and hunting season. The air was now cool and crisp. The three of them would gather once again to prepare goodies for the approaching holidays. Once again, the kitchen would fill with the wondrous scents of anise, ginger, and cinnamon. And the table would fill up with fruit cakes, light and dark, gingerbread cookies – my favorite – and jars of mincemeat. I got in on this one – it was my job to grind the mincemeat;, squish, slurp, squish it went as I turned the crank. Oh, such fun!

Now, when it came to dressing for any special occasion, my momma was always in style. Every Thursday at one o'clock, she went to see Althea, the neighborhood hair stylist. Althea knew how to make her hair look just right. On her vanity, Momma had a wide assortment of make-up, lipstick, and perfume. Her signature scent was *White Shoulders*. Momma made up for all the years of hand-me-downs, too. Her wardrobe wasn't big, at least when I was young, but it was always stylish. Her slips were *sooo silky*, the suits the perfect cut. My dad always made sure she had *sparkly* costume jewelry to set off her appearance. Then came all the accessories. There was always a RED

18

coat in the closet; her all time favorite had a black fur collar. And, if she had some extra money and could get away with it, she had matching RED shoes and a purse as well. Oh, did I mention that her favorite color was RED!!!! You may think all of this made her a very vain person. Quite the contrary, when she had herself "assembled," she was beautiful and graceful – not always easy at five feet tall – with the manners and bearing of a great *lady*.

When I turned ten, a miracle happened in our family. My little sister arrived! Oh, the joy in our home when we welcomed Susie. I dreamed forever for a sister to share my life with, just as Momma had Auntie Arvella. As we got older, Susie and I took over our dad's shopping trips at birthday time and Christmas. He would give us money and tell us what to get Momma. It was always something special and had to be hand-picked. Yes, you guessed it, usually it was also RED. I can remember having to find RED goatskin gloves- *soft* goatskin – one Christmas and then there were always RED purses, bathrobes, and nighties on the list.

Susie and I did Daddy's shopping for him because he owned his own business, the Paul-Mar Market, and had little time to shop. Momma worked by his side. He ran the meat counter and she was his cashier and supervised the help. I watched "Father Knows Best" and "Leave it to Beaver" on television during those growing up years and watched the mothers on those shows stay home all day, but not this lady. She worked hard and then came home to be my momma. She helped me with homework and went to Girl Scouts with me. She made sure I was able to take part in after school activities, and I never felt deprived. She kept our house spic and span clean and, on weekends, prepared a feast for our main meal. Whenever anyone needed her help, she was always there, and

she always made sure that Grandma and I got to church on Sunday.

The years passed and I watched Momma's hair go snow white. She sat by my grandmother's side as she passed slowly away from us with a series of strokes. She became a grandmother herself, seven times! Oh! How she loved those grandchildren. They would sit on her lap as she read stories. Now and then, she would burst into song, "Oh! Solo Mio!" Her kitchen churned out special treats, and she hugged them at every opportunity. We watched the fashions change and laughed at "mini-skirts" in the 1960s – one fad she skipped! – and then pantsuits in the 1970s. She took on the pantsuits and loved every minute! But, she knew how to dress up, and she was beautiful. Then came the day she and my dad visited us in Georgia in 1971. They drove into our yard in a brand new RED Ford Galaxy! Her long standing dream had come true – she had a RED car. My dad never missed an opportunity to spoil her or fulfill a dream. Momma and Daddy celebrated their fiftieth anniversary in 1992; Momma wore her navy blue polka dot dress suit with white pumps and a red rose corsage like the one Daddy gave her on their wedding day. They repeated their vows in a church filled with family and friends.

I told her goodbye in 2007. Susie and I sat by her bed the last three weeks of her life. During that time, we laughed and told stories. My niece Jenny came to the nursing home and gave her a manicure and painted her nails RED. We made sure her navy blue suit was clean, and we ordered her RED rose corsage.

Momma has given me so much in my life. She taught me how to be a sister, a wife, a mother, and grandmother. She showed me that family was more important than anything else in life. There were great hardships in her life, but she always kept her keen sense of humor, fortifying her and making her stronger. Through her, I have learned to appreciate the things I have and the love that I have in my life.

Her laughter still rings out today in the voices of Susie and me as we share our lives and adventures together and with our daughters.

Every now and then, as we share the kitchen or some task, we will burst forth with "Oh! Solo Mio" and we will all laugh. Our *Lady in Red* has left us a great legacy of family, home and love. My fervent prayer is that I will be able to live out my life with her grace and courage.

Zippers

It happened before I turned four years old, but I am not sure exactly when. I remember it 'cause everybody was very solemn; the lights were even kept very low. Mrs. Zimmerman, our neighbor, would come over and bring us food and talk to my grandma really soft so that I wouldn't hear. And worst of all, my momma wasn't there, and all that quiet talk was about HER! *It kinda scared me.*

But then, Daddy took me to see Momma! She was in a hospital. Everything was white and all the ladies – they called them nurses – were wearing white and they were even wearing little white hats. Momma was getting lots of rest 'cause she told me she couldn't get out of bed, and she was in some kind of contraption, and I could see that she couldn't go anywhere. Daddy lifted me up so I could give her a kiss, and then my Uncle Kenny took me downstairs again, and he played with me until Daddy came to take me home. *But Momma didn't come home for a very long time.*

But she did get better and finally came home. She had to wear a funny stiff thing they called a corset. It LOOKED awful. It had stiff "bones" that kept Momma from being able to bend down, and it had shoelaces all up the front, and Grandma would help Momma by pulling the laces REALLY tight. I wouldn't have liked that thing if I had been Momma! But then I got to see why Momma had been gone for so long. The doctors had put a ZIPPER in her back! It went all the way from below her waist almost up to her neck! *Wasn't that funny – putting a zipper in Momma's back?*

For many years after that, my momma had to go see her doctor in Detroit so he could check out her zipper. We lived thirty-two miles outside Detroit so it was a really BIG deal to go into the city; we usually made "a day" out of it. Our day always started at the doctor's office. Momma said she had to see him for a check-up. I could never go in to see the doctor; I would sit in the waiting room and watch the fish in the tank or read a book that we brought with us. Sometimes my momma's friend Faith went with us or another friend. I always figured the doctor had to unzip my momma to make sure her insides were okay.

After the doctor, we would go shopping at the big Hudson's department store. I almost always got a new dress or something pretty to wear. Then we would go to Sanders and have lunch. Of course, the big treat was the hot fudge sundae that came with lunch, and everybody went to Sanders for a sundae! (My sister Susan usually sends a jar of Sanders' fudge in her Christmas box so I can still enjoy those sundaes!) Afterwards, we would shop some more and then head back to Plymouth until our next visit.

I had grown up some before I was finally told more about the "zipper" in Momma's back. You see, she broke her back and they had to fuse her spine at the waist. It meant she couldn't bend from the waist, and it meant she spent most of her life in pain from her back. Our visits to the doctor in Detroit were for shots that she took in her spine to help control that pain. I only saw the doctor give her one shot when I was a young teenager and I almost passed out. I will never know how she withstood that pain. But eventually she didn't need to go to Detroit or to have the shots any more. There were new medications, and there were new therapies.

Momma spent most of her adult years working beside my dad in their grocery stores or in meat markets. When they finally left their last business, she went to work as a cashier for Kroger super markets. That put her on her feet eight to ten hours every day, and it took a heavy toll on her. She developed osteoarthritis in her spine as well as osteoporosis. By the time she was 56 years old, she had to quit working because her back could not withstand the pressures any longer. After retirement, she and my dad took walks and she remained active, although more sedentary. She kept the pace up until Daddy passed away in 1997.

A year later, she moved her body the wrong way in the shower. Something snapped. Her arthritic spine began to crumble. She had surgery, but her spine was too brittle to hold the rods – she would never walk again on her own. Susie and I had always teased her about the "zipper" in her back – the scar that held her together. She always laughed as if it meant nothing when, in all reality, it had meant so much to the way she lived her life – with courage.

Going to Grandpa's House

There's a song we used to sing that started out, "Over the river and through the woods to Grandmother's house we go." I always think of that song when I remember our trips to Grandma and Grandpa Fielden's house in Tennessee.

Traveling in the 1950s was very different from traveling today. For one thing, our roads and highways were nowhere as efficient as today. The roads between Detroit and Knoxville, Tennessee, were mostly two lane roads that wound through every small town and through some very steep mountains. Especially in the mountains, there were no shoulders either. It was usually straight up the mountain on one side and straight down into the valley on the other side! If someone broke down on the road or had an accident, you would sit in "parked" traffic and heat for hours! No Fun! There were a couple of things that were fun, though. One was seeing all the barns that had "See Rock City" painted on their roofs and the other was all the signs painted on the rock sides in the mountains. Things like, "The end of the world is at hand!" and "Jesus loves you!" One of the scariest sights for me, but also

fun, was seeing an occasional black bear in the mountains. They would come right up to the car if you stopped but we would always keep the windows up tight and stay in the car!

Another difference in traveling was the lack of rest stops. The highways didn't have rest stops with bathrooms and picnic tables. Instead, you had to take your chances with gas station restrooms along the way. And believe me, they weren't any fun at all! They didn't even have indoor facilities at all the gas stations, using "outhouses" instead. Ooowhee they stunk and were filthy. I actually got so I could ride all the way from Detroit to Tennessee without going to the bathroom!

Today it takes only nine hours to get from Detroit to Knoxville but in the 1950s, it took more like eighteen to twenty-four hours. We usually did not try to drive straight through like we do now; instead, we would stop for the night at a motel – or what was billed as a motel. Usually, they were little cabins – one room with a bathroom. They usually smelled really musty from being closed up and they were stuffy- no air-conditioning back then, either! Not even a fan!

The roads through Michigan and Ohio took you through industrial cities with their smokestacks and factories and then through flat countryside dotted with farms. But once we got to Kentucky and Tennessee, the roadside scenery began to change as well. There were fewer large cities and far less industry. Instead, there were small farms that looked much poorer than Ohio. The houses seemed older and tired with rusty metal roofs and broken-down fences. People began to advertise with self-painted signs – frequently misspelled – and roadside stands. The wares they had were different as well. There were homemade jams and jellies, honey, quilts hanging on lines, and all kinds of little trinkets like plaster statues of Jesus or painted dogs. "Dog Patch" was always a highlight of any trip, and I would plead to stop and buy a souvenir. It seemed to me, we had entered a whole new world.

I would sit in the backseat of the car and marvel at all the changes and differences from my regular world. The mountains were beautiful, but the roads were scary and I would hang on to the arm rests for fear we would fall off the road! And then, we would leave the "main" road, and suddenly the world would open up and we would be crossing Norris Dam! Oh, how beautiful! We were up over the sparkling water, and the HUGE manmade lake was surrounded by trees and greenery. It was a gorgeous sight, and I also knew that the long trip was almost over. We were not far from Grandma and Grandpa's now!

Once across the dam, the road became even narrower, and we could reach out of the car and touch the overhanging limbs of the trees. It was a beautiful and amazing ride. Finally, the car would slow down, and there was the road sign – Hinds Creek. Dad would turn onto the old dirt road and we would start into the real "backwoods."

Now the road began to climb and to wind through old farms. It seemed every farmer in every field and every person sitting on a porch would wave at our car as we drove along, and Daddy would wave back. The road was rough and full of holes as we bumped along. My heart would start to beat harder as the excitement began to build. Finally, we saw the church where we turned, and just past the church was the old barn at the side of the road as we drove through the bubbling creek bed that crossed the road. One final climb and there was Aunt Georgie's house, and she would run out and wave as we started around the curve and there, on the side of the hill, was Grandma and Grandpa's house. Almost always, they were sitting on the porch waiting for us!

The reunion was sweet and the hugs were strong and loving! Grandpa would lift me into the air and rub his stubbly beard against my face. The sweet smell of tobacco filled my nose as I laughed and pleaded to get down, only to be taken into grandma's arms and hugged some more. For the next week, I would be spoiled rotten by these wonderful, country folk, and the memories we made would last a lifetime.

These images no longer exist as the new interstates have emerged with their modern rest stops and chain motels and restaurants. We still travel through the awesome mountains, but they pass by quickly and there are very few narrow hairpin turns. As for the people on Hinds Creek, many are still there or their children and grandchildren, but many have moved to the city. Little did I know as a child that all of those waving to us from their fields and porches were related to us and that they were welcoming my dad home. Home to the fields of his youth and where Paul Fielden stood as a local folk hero – another story for another day.

Tall Tale of a Mountain Man

William Paris Fielden NEVER knew that was his name! He always thought his name was Billy Paris Fielden and that is what is printed on his tombstone. Billy was my grandfather, born and raised in the foothills of the Great Smoky Mountains, just outside of Knoxville, Tennessee.

Grandpa was a tall man, about six feet two inches. They say he had dark hair, but I never saw it. It was always a thick mane of snow atop his head. His eyes twinkled and you knew he was full of the dickens. When he laughed, it was full and deep – and he loved to laugh. His face was always stubbly, and he liked to rub it against my face. There was always the sweet smell of fresh tobacco about him – he always had a "chaw" in his mouth or one nearby. He and Grandma used to sit on their front porch in their rockers and have "spittin" contests with their "tobacca."

Getting to Grandpa's house was always an adventure. His farm was way back in the "holler" on Hinds Creek. The road was narrow and winding – steep on one side and straight down on the other. At one point, you drove through the creek, no bridges here! In the spring time, the valley was a wonderland with the white, delicate blooms of the dogwood trees. In a rainstorm, the creek became a mean and angry river. People along the way would be sitting on their porches and wave as you went by, whether they recognized you or not. They were just friendly folk.

As a child, I loved to sit and listen to the adults talking and telling stories about Grandpa's adventures and those of my dad and his brothers, Ken and Ray. They would talk of the times that Grandpa would gather the produce from the farmers in the "holler" and drive into town to sell – first by wagon and later using a pick-up truck. My dad liked to ride into town with him, always hoping for a sweet treat.

The family grew up during the Depression when times were tough. But there was another situation that occurred at about the same time – Prohibition. And back in the hills and hollers of Tennessee, a new industry grew and prospered – MOONSHINE. It became a new crop for the Fielden clan. Grandpa ran the still while his two oldest sons, Paul (my dad) and Ken, ran the moonshine into town. There came a day when the "revenuers" found Grandpa and his still. He took off running and, as he ran, his overalls, always worn loose, fell down around his ankles, tripping him and sending him head over heels! Well, that escapade gave him time to get some rest – behind bars! Meanwhile, the boys kept the business going until he returned.

In the 1950s, he and Grandma lived on a large dairy farm. Grandma churned fresh butter every morning to spread on warm biscuits. I can still hear the paddle as it thumped against the floor of the porch. In addition to the dairy cows, there was a large tobacco barn, honey bees and hives, and lots of chickens everywhere you went. I was the "citified" grandchild, and my other cousins were used to visiting the farm often. Grandpa always enjoyed getting the chickens to chase ME around the yard or having me ride his mule Sam. There came a day, though, when Sam took it upon himself to close me in the "outhouse." He backed himself up to the door and wouldn't move! I could hear Grandpa laughing from the

porch – I could never prove it, but I suspected that Sam had some HELP!

We took Grandma and Grandpa to town one day to do some shopping. Grandma liked all kinds of "geegaws" – glass ornaments like chicken shaped butter dishes. She and Grandpa were in a back corner of the store when we heard the sound of breaking glass. Before we could even take a breath, here came my grandparents with Grandpa pushing Grandma every step of the way – "Come on now, hurry. We can't stop. Hurry on up!" It seems Grandma had broken a dish and Grandpa wasn't about to pay for something that was broken, so he was running for his life! Laughing every step of the way!

Now there was one phenomenon that shattered all of our eardrums and it seemed to be a family trait – at least with Grandpa, my dad, and my Uncle Kenny. However, Grandpa was the ALL TIME CHAMP. We would be sitting in the living room and suddenly, Grandpa would sneeze. Maybe I should say his WHOLE BODY SNEEZED! His feet came off the floor, his arms flew up into the air, and his entire body rocked backward. And the NOISE! It shook the whole house – we always checked to make sure the roof was still in place. He really enjoyed his sneezes.

I loved this old man. I loved it when he asked me to give him some "sugar" or tickled my face with that stubbly beard. He was a genuine individual who lived life HIS way. He didn't have to put on "airs" or try to impress anyone. We were stationed in Italy when we lost him. My dad didn't want to tell me what happened, but my mom thought I should know.

The family had decided that Grandpa, now 82, was getting too old to live by himself out in the "holler." They made arrangements for him to move into a mobile home in my Uncle Bill's trailer park. That way my Aunt Evelyn, my dad's sister, could keep tabs on him. He was going to move on Saturday morning. When my cousin Harold went to help him get ready that morning, he found him in bed. The coroner said he died about 6:00 that morning, by his own hand. Billy Paris Fielden had decided his own fate, the way he had always done. I don't believe in suicide, but in this case, I have always thought...

Billy Paris Fielden died as he had lived – GENUINELY

My Imaginary Friends

Were you ever alone, needing a friend? Someone you could talk to? Maybe play with? Tell your secrets to? Someone who was always available, just for you? Someone who could always go with you, wherever you went? Well, I did.

I was an only child, very loved and very indulged back in the late 1940's and early 1950's. It's true, I usually had my Grandma close by to tell me stories and play games with me. But, I spent a lot of time alone, with no one to play with at all. And so, I made up a secret friend, not just one but really three!

My friends and I had soooo much fun! Our favorite game was playing cowboys and Indians. We would ride the wild west, "Getty up, Getty up!" We would chase the bad guys and put them in jail. The Indians would attack and we would chase them back, but usually we were friends. Sometimes we were the Indians, sitting by our fires or in our wigwams. I would carry my papoose on my back as I walked through our village. I would make tents out of blankets, using the table or the chairs to support my tents. Now and then I was allowed to sleep in my tents with my imaginary friends. They also came to all my tea parties, visiting with my dolls and teddy bear and enjoying the tea and cookies. (Grandma always made sure there enough cookies for them.)

The back seat of our car was quite crowded when we all got in. My Momma and Daddy didn't mind taking them along but sometimes Daddy got upset when they were slow getting into the car. I would point out things to them as we drove along, they were from another time and really didn't recognize everything in my real world. We would pretend that we were in a race with other cars on the road and of course, we always won! They likened those car races to chasing bad guys back in the old west.

I was always glad that they were around when I got scared. That wasn't often but it was nice during really bad storms when the thunder and lightening were loud and banging. When Momma was in the hospital, I was really afraid and they kept me company and kept me from crying because I really missed my Momma. And I always knew that no one could take me away from my family because they would protect me.

My secret friends were very well known, its just that no one realized that they were my "special friends." Once a week, they could be heard on the radio, later on the television. You see, my special friends were the Lone Ranger, Tonto and a horse named Silver!

They disappeared one day, about the time I started school. It seems I didn't need them anymore. Now I had real friends to play with and tell my secrets to. They just rode off into the sunset and I never saw them again!

Hi Ho Silver…. Away!

Growing Up on Pacific

My family moved to 799 Pacific Avenue, Plymouth, Michigan, in the spring of 1952. I was six years old at the time. Our new house was larger than our old house had been. This one had two bedrooms - the smaller one for my parents and the larger one for me to share with my Grandma Lidgard. The living room had a large picture window with the most awful drapes! They were dark green with HUGE birds on them. Our furniture was dark green and the carpet had BIG flowers. I've always wondered about my mom's decorating tastes at that time in her life! There was a kitchen large enough for us to eat in. The basement was a wonderful playground for me with Momma's new electric washing machine, complete with a wringer and a fruit cellar that doubled as a tornado cellar. And there was a play area set up there just for me.

There were probably twenty houses on the "top" block of Pacific Avenue. We were the "top" block because our street was a hill and we were at the top of the hill, which was perfect for coasting downhill in wagons, on bikes, on roller skates, and even sleds. Just about every house on the street had kids, and those that didn't had grandchildren that came to visit and play. We played in and out of our friends' houses while our moms kept track of our general movements – it was safe and it was fun.

That first summer on Pacific was a busy one for my family. My cousin Carol, who lived in Arizona, but was getting married in Plymouth.

It was really exciting for me because I was going to be the flower girl in her wedding. My Mom was making my dress, so I spent a lot of time being measured for my dress, making sure the sleeves fit, the skirt fit and the hem was just right! But I loved my dress and I felt like a princess. The dress was a soft lavender with a silk and net skirt. I was beautiful when I put it on!

Now, my adventures with my friends were many and varied by the seasons. Television was brand new and did not really cater to children. We did have a few favorite programs like *Howdy Doody*, *Kukla Fran and Ollie, and the Lone Ranger*. We spent most of our time playing outside. We didn't have to come home until the street lights came on.

During the summer, two or three of us had wading pools and we would take turns playing in each one of them, pretending that each pool was some new and exciting place, such as a watering hole in the great African desert with lions and elephants coming to drink, or maybe it was the Everglades where hungry alligators threatened us at every turn.

Afternoons might find us building tents on the clotheslines using old blankets and sheets. Our tents would take up an entire wash line. Sometimes our tents were in the old west as we rested our wagon train, and other times they were exotic tents from "Arabian Nights." And, there were the times when they were our homes where we practiced being parents with our dolls and cooking for our men – yes, the boys joined in as well, going off to work and coming home for dinner (they would really go off and play whatever boys played!).

We became entrepreneurs with our lemonade and Kool Aid stands. Our counter was usually made of orange crates from my dad's store.

The orange crates were divided wooden shipping crates for oranges. A toy cash register held our dividends which, more often than not, turned out to be less than what we spent to set up the stand! But we would close up our stand and went off to the store to buy a candy bar, always proud of our effort and success.

The railroad tracks were close by and frequently provided a day's pleasure as we packed a snack lunch and hiked along the tracks. Sometimes we would find the fire pits where hoboes had spent a night and cooked their meal. Other times we would stop and hunt for pollywogs and frogs in the small ponds in the fields near the track. Mr. Goebel and the Twin Pines dairy truck made its daily trip through our neighborhood. Back then, the trucks did not have refrigeration; they kept the milk cool by using large blocks of ice. We would chase the truck down the street and "plead" with Mr. Goebel to give us a chunk of ice. He usually kept us waiting for two or three stops before he "gave in" and gave us each a chunk of ice.

About the time we turned six years old, we all seemed to get our new two-wheele bikes.With those bikes, our freedom became complete! We could now explore the streets around us, riding around the block onto Evergreen or Arthur streets, and we could go to the park two blocks over on Auburn. Ohh! The feel of freedom, riding your bike with the wind in your hair as you flew up and down the two hills on our street, then

walking your bike back up the hill. As we grew older, we were able to ride our bikes up to the high school for afternoon free swims in the school pool or for cooking and sewing classes in summer school. Saturday afternoon matinees at the theater became possible and "shopping" for candy at a local corner market. We were so grown up on our bikes!

The playground on Auburn ran during the afternoon on weekdays during the summer. The counselors were college or high school kids hired by the Recreation Department and trained to provide programs to younger kids – like us! We enjoyed all kinds of arts and crafts from plaster-of-paris molds to making pot holders on looms. We would take our treasures home to our moms who would proudly display them somewhere in the house. Baseball, kickball, and tag were fun games when there were enough kids present to play. And then, there were the hotly contested competitions to see who had the biggest, prettiest, smallest cat, dog, doll or whatever. We had dress-up contests, too. There always seemed to be something to do.

The biggest treat of the summer, of course, was the Good Humor man. He would ring the bells on the front of his truck, and we would run for our allowance or our parents to plead for a treat. My favorite was always the toasted almond ice cream bar, but he also had creamsicles, Eskimo pies, nutty ice cream cones, fudgesicles, and so many more treats made for the express purpose of thrilling kids of ALL ages!

But my favorite summer memory was a quiet time I spent alone. I would lay down in the cool grass and clover in my front yard. Lying on my tummy, I would search through the clover for that elusive four-leaf clover for good luck – now and then I would actually find one. Or maybe I would lie on my back, looking at the clouds and dreaming about tomorrow… I would watch the clouds and find all the shapes. It was usually a quiet time in late afternoon under picture perfect blue skies with the locusts humming in the trees…

Fall saw all of us troop off to Bird Elementary School on Sheldon Road. The school was one of two new schools that had been opened in 1952 in order to accommodate the first wave of "baby-boomers" – the generation spawned by returning World War II soldiers. We had to walk the ten blocks to the school, but as we grew older, we were able to ride our bikes.

At home, we raked the autumn leaves and played in the giant piles formed by our effort. The leaves became forts, like the Alamo, or castles where great kings lived. We staged great battles between the cowboys and Indians as well as sword fights that saved the princess and her kingdom. At the end of the day, an adult would join us to burn the leaves, usually bringing marshmallows for us to roast. I can still smell the leaves burning in the crisp autumn air…

The first snowflakes of winter usually fell by mid-November. What excitement that first snowfall brought with its sparkling flakes and clear cold air of winter. We would rush outside to make snowmen and snow angels. With boys in the group, we also had to make snow forts which became fierce battlegrounds between the boys and the girls. By Christmas, the lakes would be frozen solid and we would plead with our parents to take us to Wilcox Lake so we could ice skate. Afterward, we would rush home for steaming hot cocoa and cookies in the warmth of Momma's kitchen.

We kept ourselves busy inside as well during those long, cold winters. There were always lots of games to play, like Monopoly, Sorry and card games. Bonnie, my best friend, and I always had an abundance of paper dolls to keep us entertained for hours on end.

The first breath of springtime took us back outside. Baseball bats, balls, and mitts came out from under our beds or out of our closets as we took to the street for our first game of the year. The gutter grate was first base, the manhole cover was second base, and the gutter grate on the other side of the street became third base. Home plate was usually a piece of a cardboard box. These same bases worked well for kickball too! Of course, we could always play jump rope and laugh at the boys or play marbles and get beaten by the boys. And then there were the newly blossoming trees, just right for climbing!

We never missed an opportunity to use up every minute of the day! Our stage plays were STUPENDOUS, our athletic prowess was LEGENDARY, and our energy BOUNDLESS! The friendships we made would never end, or so it seemed. But the memories we made on Pacific, THEY WILL LIVE FOREVER IN OUR HEARTS.

Ghosts...Goblins...and Spooks in the Night

Halloween in Plymouth, Michigan in the 1950s was exciting and fun! It wasn't just an evening event but a full day of fun and excitement. We would leave for school in the morning, carefully carrying our costumes in a bag along with our lunch. All morning we tried sooo hard to focus on our schoolwork, but it was nearly impossible. Lunchtime would finally arrive and we would quickly eat our lunches, and **THEN** we would get into our costumes....*Finally!* Class by class we would line up, the high school band would arrive, and we would start our parade. The parade route went two blocks up Ann Arbor Trail, then turned into the neighborhood where we would walk one block over to Maple Street and then we walked the two blocks back to Bird Elementary School. The people in their homes came out to watch and take pictures and our parents stood on the street to watch. We loved every minute of the fun and attention! When we got back to the school, it was *PARTY* time!

Never was the walk home as fun as it was on Halloween. The air was cool and crisp, the leaves crunched under our feet and... *there was something spooky in the air.* The next couple hours dragged on endlessly as we waited for sunset and the bewitching hour. Momma always made chili for dinner on Halloween; it was warm and filling. Finally, it was dark and we all went out and lit our pumpkins and turned on our porch lights. There were kids in almost every house in the neighborhood, and we knew our haul for the night would be huge. Our neighborhood was four blocks long from Junction street to Williams and eight streets from Sheldon Road to Harvey Street. We were allowed to go on our street, Pacific, and Evergreen Street behind us.

Our costumes back then were fun as well. When I was real little, my momma always bought my costumes. They seemed to be made of a gauzy material and always had a real neat mask to go with them. One year, my costume was a scary witch. I wore a black dress and a black cape. There was a pointy black hat and my mask had a long pointy nose with warts on it. Another year, I was a devil! The costume was red and had a long tail with an arrow at its end. My mask was rubber and had these ugly horns sticking out. As we got older, we began to make our costumes. My first homemade costume was "Mrs. Got Rocks," my momma's name for women who showed off their wealth. I dressed up in one of my grandma's dresses, gloves, hat, and lots of jewelry. Momma made up my face like a grown-up lady. I was something else! Another costume that I really liked was my hobo costume. I wore a pair of Daddy's old pants, a white shirt, a pillow belly, and suspenders. I used coal to make a beard and stubble on my face. With an old hat and a bandana pack on a stick, I was pretty nifty!

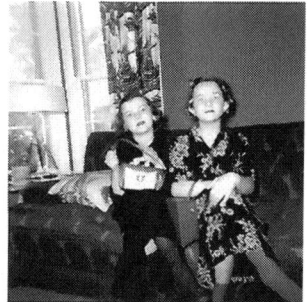

My best friend Bonnie's older sister Janice was our chaperone as we set out on our Halloween trek. "Trick or Treat" could be heard up and down the street as groups of kids filled their bags with goodies. And the treats were plentiful...full size Milky Ways, Butterfingers,

Clark Bars, Zagnuts...ummm good. There were homemade popcorn balls with caramel or gooey Karo syrup, candy, and homemade chocolate chip cookies, apples, and candy apples on a stick. More and more goodies...Turkish taffy, Chuckles, Necco Wafers, Mary Janes, Slo Pokes, and bubble gum. Our bags filled and got heavy. There was always a brand new toothbrush in the bag... Harry's dad was a dentist. Someone usually added pennies to our bags and we thought we were rich. By the time we went the full length of our street and back to the top, we were usually so worn out we couldn't go another step! As we got older, our trick or treating area grew and we could go almost anywhere in town. Sometimes, I would also go out with my cousin Ruthann. Her older sister Roberta would take us into her neighborhood for more goodies.

Of course, there were always things happening along the way. There was one house on the third block of our street that always was very *Spooky!* It was all decorated out front and in the living room, and there was scary music playing on their record player. The family was all dressed up and the dad would invite us "into his parlor" where he would demand a "trick" or "treat." We'd always have to sing a song, do a dance or do something for our treat. He made it lots of fun to get our treat, and he always gave the greatest treats!

Then there was the year my grandma had a really *SCARY* Halloween. It seems we had a wonderful cat at our house. His name was Bootsie, and he was all black with four white paws and a white collar and belly – we called it his tuxedo. On Halloween, we always put him in the basement for his safety. Then came this special Halloween where Grandma was at home alone handing out the treats while I was trick or treating. A bunch of kids came to the door, and with them, there was **THE** cat. It upset Grandma that Bootsie had managed to escape. So, she managed to recapture him and put him back in the basement. I came home and trick or treating ended and all was quiet in our house. Suddenly, in the basement, there was this horrible "Screeching" – *SPOOKY!* We raced to the basement, and lo and behold, there were the two cats, hair standing straight up, backs arched, hissing and screeching at each other! Well, that wouldn't do! I managed to capture Bootsie and Grandma captured the visiting cat and put him outside again. Afterwards, we sat and laughed at our Halloween adventure.

Ghosts...and Goblins... and Spooks in the Night! Halloween was fun and left wonderful memories. We were safe walking the streets in our neighborhood; our neighbors made it fun and spooky for us. It was truly a time of innocence, and we were allowed as children to experience the night and enjoy ourselves.

Santa? Is that You?

It was the perfect Christmas Eve. The sky was crystal clear with all the stars twinkling brightly. Daddy even took me outside to look at the stars to prove to me that Santa wasn't going to have any trouble finding our house. There was about a foot of snow on the ground; Daddy had shoveled the walks when he got home from work. My Uncle Kenny and Aunt Billie came out from Detroit and were planning to spend the night with us. And Aunt Betty and Uncle Walt had come over to party with us while we waited for Santa. I was the only kid, and I was enjoying all of the attention.

The year was 1952, and I was six years old that Christmas. I was soooo excited about Santa. My Christmas list had been pretty simple – I wanted a new doll and a bright red sled! If Santa brought the sled, I knew I could talk Daddy into taking me to the park to go sledding tomorrow. I was sure!

Well, Momma and Daddy and my aunts and uncles partied and had a good time. They were laughing a lot and drinking what they called "Christmas Cheer." They wouldn't let me have any, but then Grandma and I had fizzy ginger ale that tickled our noses and all the cookies we could eat!

We had a brand new television that year – *our first one ever*. It was playing Christmas shows with people like Jack Benny, Milton Berle, and Red Skelton – *I really didn't like them* – but Momma, Daddy, and my aunts and uncles thought they were funny and they had good singers on their shows. At 9:00 PM, the news people broke into the show and announced that Santa had been spotted over Detroit and good little girls and boys better get to bed. **WELL**, I wasn't going to let Santa miss **MY** house, so I gave out hugs and kisses to everyone and scrambled off to bed.

Wasn't I just the perfect little kid? Ha! I was going to fool everyone and stay awake until Santa got there! So, with great determination, I set about staying awake. The laughter continued in the living room, and Grandma kept checking to make sure I was going to sleep. I'd make sure my eyes were closed and I'd stay real still. When she left, I'd sit back up and look out the window. My bedroom window was on the front of the house and looked out on the street where all the cars were parked. Then...

I could tell it was real late. Aunt Betty and Uncle Walt left. Momma, Daddy, Uncle Kenny, and Aunt Billie all began to whisper. Grandma came to stand by my bedroom door – I think she was the lookout. The front door opened *very quietly.* **He was here at last, Santa was here!** I peeked out my window, just a crack. And what did I see? Well, it wasn't a sleigh with eight tiny reindeer, that's for sure. It was none other than my daddy! And he was carrying my brand new red sled up the front walk and into **OUR HOUSE!** *Was my daddy really Santa?* Was I going to tell him I saw him and my sled?

I was really going to have to think this one over before tomorrow morning...

Next morning I popped up bright and early! I decided I didn't want to spoil Momma and Daddy's Christmas – *I wasn't sure I would get any more presents either.* There, under the tree were all my wonderful presents from Santa! A brand new doll that I promptly named Bubbles because she had chubby cheeks. A new toy box to keep everything in, and there, leaning against the wall, was my new red flyer sled! It even had a tag on it that said, "To Sandy, from Santa" –

in my momma's handwriting!

I didn't tell Momma and Daddy that I knew who Santa was that year. I actually dragged the news out for two more Christmases. *No one ever accused me of being stupid!* When I finally told them, we all had a good laugh. Two years later, I had a new baby sister in my house, and I became Santa's helper and then Santa. But you know, as long as I lived at home, Santa always found a way to leave a special surprise under the tree. Just for me.

Forever Friends

Summer 1954 started like any other summer, but it became a summer of excitement and change for me. A new family moved in two houses down from mine and they had a daughter my age. Her name was Bonnie Howitz, and together we would form a friendship that would last a lifetime.

Bonnie's family was very different from mine. She had an older sister, Janice, who was ten years older than Bonnie and me. Her dad worked in a factory and her mom was a school cook. I remember that her dad was really tall and he had a really deep voice and a wonderful laugh. Her mom was soft spoken. They became a second family for me.

Bonnie and I became fast friends from the start. We were the same age, eight, and in the same grade. We seemed to like all the same things and played together every day. We were even on the same party line and, if we picked the phone up at the same time, we could talk to each other without going through the operator! That way we could make our plans for the day.

We both collected paper dolls and loved playing with them. We would walk uptown with Janice to find the newest set of paper dolls. All the movie stars had paper dolls with beautiful dresses to wear – Elizabeth Taylor, Rosemary Clooney, Shirley Temple, and Marilyn Monroe. Bonnie and I would lay out our dolls and their dresses and play all afternoon. It got to the point that one day, we laid out all our paper dolls and they took up one half of Bonnie's basement! I don't know what was funny that day, but we began laughing and couldn't stop. We rolled all over those paper dolls, laughing until our sides hurt!

There was one day that we decided to bake bread. It couldn't be hard, we saw our moms do it all the time. We spent the afternoon at Bonnie's house mixing the dough. We'd add yeast and flour, lots of flour. Then we had to let it rise. All the while, Janice stood in the background saying, "I don't think you should be doing this. I don't think Momma will like this!" There was flour all over the kitchen, and when the yeast began to "rise" we had dough and batter all over the kitchen — the counters were covered, the floor was covered, and the oven was a total disaster! We were trying to clean it up when Bonnie's mom came home. But I was chicken and I ran out the back door — I knew she was going to be terribly angry and she was! I knew that I had escaped just in time, or so I thought. Mrs. Howitz called my mom, and then I really caught it. Bonnie and I couldn't play together for a whole week!

Bonnie and I liked to explore things. We lived near railroad tracks, and it was fun to "hike" over there and walk along the tracks. There were all kinds of wonders there. Hoboes used to ride the trains then, and we would find empty food cans and the remnants of fires where they had cooked their meals. We never saw a hobo, but we knew they had been there. There were small ponds in the field before the train tracks, and we would take empty jars and collect pollywogs (baby frogs) in the jars and take them home. Of course, we always had to let them go, our moms weren't as thrilled with them as we were! There was an alley that ran behind our houses where the garbage trucks would go once a week to pick up our trash. Well, Bonnie and I explored the alley. too, looking under the garbage cans for crickets and roly-poly bugs. We'd capture them too, and take them home, BUT they never made it into the house! One day when we were exploring the alley, we found a rope swing at one of the houses. I sat on the swing and twisted and twisted the rope. It would be fun when I let it go and the swing untwisted, whirling me round and round 'til I got dizzy. Only thing was, I had long hair that caught in the twisting rope and I was slowly hanging myself! Bonnie ran home and got her mom, who brought scissors and cut my hair to free me! No more long hair and no more twisting in swings!

During the summer, we would ride our bikes up to the high school to take summer classes. In the morning, we would take swimming lessons from Mr. McFall. He was the high school swim coach, but he gave summer classes in the big high school pool. Afternoons found us back at the pool for open swim. We also took home-economic classes during the summer in the high school home-ec rooms. There would be cooking classes and sewing classes. I never did very well in the sewing classes – they foretold my future in junior high classes yet to come!

We went places with my mom. One trip was to see my Auntie Arvella. She lived on a lake in the Waterloo Recreation Area. There was a popular song at the time and called *Waterloo*. Bon and I started singing, "Waterloo, Waterloo! Where are you, my Waterloo!" at the top of our lungs! We all laughed and sang on 'til we reached my aunt's house. The rest of the day was spent swimming, eating and swimming some more.

Bonnie and I rode our bikes everywhere. We'd ride them over to the playground on Auburn, two blocks away. We'd race them there and home, and we'd race up and down our street. Bill's Market in lower town was just a few blocks away, and we'd ride there in summer to get popsicles and candy. Bird Elementary School was only 10 blocks away. We'd ride our bikes to and from school when the weather allowed. When we were thirteen, I moved to Lake Pointe Village, a new subdivision just outside of town. Bonnie would ride out to my house for the day and we would meet half-way and ride together out to my house.

Our very favorite past-time though was the movies. Janice would walk us uptown to one of the theaters – the Penn or the P&A. And there we would fall in love each weekend with our favorite movie stars, living through their angst, their love, and their battles. We saw some of the great classic movies together – An Affair to Remember, Tammy, Love Me Tender, Ben Hur, Pillow Talk, and so many more. Our love of movies has never dimmed. We still go to see a movie or watch one on television, whenever we get a chance. We just live farther apart now – Michigan and Florida.

Our adventures have changed in adulthood, but they have continued. However, that is another story for another day. Just let it be known that this friendship, started at the age of eight, has grown into something much more important as the years have grown. Bonnie and I have become forever friends – forever sisters.

Whoaaa, Nellie!!

SHE was already sixty-six years old when we met. SHE already had grey hair and walked slowly. Her back was distinguished by the "widow's hump" – a disfiguration caused by osteoporosis – that made it look like she was walking stooped over. SHE had already raised eight children of her own, and I was her twenty-eighth grandchild. So, our first meeting was not really auspicious. There was absolutely nothing on February 8, 1946, that hinted at the special bond we would share or the ties that would bind us together for all of my life. SHE was my grandmother, Nellie Scott Lidgard.

Grandma Lidgard had seen her share of life. Born on the prairie, she had ridden in covered wagons, watched the first automobiles take to the road, and flown in airplanes across the country. Five sons and three daughters had shown her that nothing was unimaginable, and anything was possible. She had been a mother, grandmother, great-grandmother – a barber, a mid-wife, a grocer, a farmer, and a hospital dietician. Now, at sixty-six, she was retired, that is until I came along and she became my babysitter! It was now my mother's turn to work, and because Grandma lived at our house, she got her newest granddaughter to watch over.

The stories started even before I was old enough to remember, about the time I could sit up on her lap and sit still for more than a minute. She told me about this little girl, Caroline, who just couldn't mind her momma. One day she decided to follow her dad into town – a two day trip back and forth. Well, little Caroline followed him out onto the prairie and then couldn't find her way home! Her momma called in the neighbors and her brothers, and they went lookin'. But no one found Caroline. All night Momma paced the floor and worried about her Caroline. Late the next day, when Dad came home, he found Caroline out on the prairie waitin' for him and pulled her up into the cart for the ride down the lane to the farm. WHAT a welcome he got when he came in with Caroline!! He didn't know she'd raised an uproar and been missing all night. Well, Caroline got lots of hugs and lots of tears and then she got her dad's hand on her little backside!! Moral of the story my Grandma said – ALWAYS do what Momma tells you and NEVER leave Momma's sight. The story was real, and Caroline was Nellie's mom.

It was sooo warm and the winds were dry. Reminded Grandma of another time and place, she said. It was a time when she was just a little girl. The family had ventured away from Indiana and all they knew to settle in Nebraska. The

trip was a long one and hard in their covered wagon, and she had had to walk part of the way. At last they had settled in Nebraska, and her dad had built a "soddy" for them to live in. A "soddy" was a house built of mud and grass with a dirt floor, common on the prairie during the 1800s. It was nothing like their house had been in Indiana. This house had only one room for all of them to live in. Her dad had managed to clear land and get a planting in, but then came the long, hot summer with a blistering sun and those awful dry winds. Then, one day, Dad had come running in, yelling at everyone to get into the soddy and bring water. He dropped down the windows and had them all wet down a rag. Then he told them to pray. They stayed in the soddy as the blistering prairie fire swept over them, burning everything in its path. But the soddy stood, and the family inside remained safe. They returned to Indiana as soon as they could put their meager belongings together.

And the stories continued, with tales of gypsies and dances, funny characters and life as she had known it. But not only did she bring me a wealth of stories, she brought me a world of fun and laughter, even on my darkest days.

Back in the 1950s the measles were serious business. You had to stay in bed in a dark room for days and days and days! But, if you had a super special grandma at your house, time went by faster with stories and GAMES. Did you know that buttons were magic? I found that out when the measles hit my house. I was moaning and groaning about my fate when my grandma brought a jar of buttons into my room. There were big buttons, tiny buttons, sparkly buttons, and buttons of every description. She dumped them on my bed and said, "Let's play." It so happened that my bed was covered with a homemade quilt with the wedding ring pattern – intertwined circles. It became a bedsize game board! My buttons chased hers all around that quilt, taking them and losing them, all afternoon. Before I knew it, it was dinnertime, and I felt a lot better.

The next day started out B-O-R-I-N-G again. But, again, my Grandma came in and asked if I was ready for a game of hide and seek. How? I couldn't leave my bed OR my room. Easy. "I'll think of a place to hide, and you have to guess where I am hiding." We played hide and seek all day, or so it seemed. There were all kinds of places to hide in your imagination – the hamper, the milk chute, behind the curtains, in the linen closet. It was wondrous! Years later, after Grandma had suffered a stroke and could no longer get around easily, we played that game again while she sat in her favorite red chair and I sat beside her on the floor. What fun we had!

There were times when my mom and my grandma did not agree on the rules governing one Sandy. In those cases, Grandma became my conspirator! Television was in its early days back then. "I Love Lucy" was everyone's favorite show, including mine. However, it came on after my bedtime. Grandma and I shared the bedroom next to the living room, and the television sat in the corner opposite our bedroom door. So, on nights when "I Love Lucy" came on, Grandma would get up to go to the restroom, and, as she went by our door, she would crack it open just far enough for me to lie on the end of the bed and watch the show. When it was over, she reversed the process!

Sometimes I think my mom knew all about it, but she never let on. It was Grandma's and my secret.

Grandma shared her wit and her fun with my friends as well. She was a constant in our home, so she couldn't help but get to know the kids around us. One of our favorite games, especially on days when we couldn't play outside, was to play pioneers in the basement. We would sit on the lower basement steps with a rope in our hands and guide our horses and buckboards west across the prairie. Grandma didn't usually take part in these games; she let us use our imaginations to settle the west. But one day she was sweeping the landing at the top of the stairs, and our buckboard was getting away. My friend Bonnie yelled out to the horses, "WHOA, Nellie!" and my very droll Grandma answered, "I don't want to whoa, I've got a long way to go!"

And so she did. Nellie Scott Lidgard lived to be eighty-two years old. She lived with us until I was fourteen and she was eighty. During those years, she watched the early jet trails across the sky and listened to the first sonic booms. Her family grew in size as she added four more grandchildren, and her great-grandchildren began arriving in fast succession. She never lost her sense of humor nor her imagination. It would be many years before I realized that the stories she told me were true; they were the stories of her life. Of all her grandchildren, she left me with the most precious gift – her love, her imagination, and the memories of her life. WHOAAA, Nellie – her story still goes on, and now someone who loved her greatly will write it down for all to hear.

The Big Yellow Bowl

Growing up in the 1950s, it is a sure thing that almost every kitchen contained a set of Pyrex mixing bowls. Our kitchen was no different. The smallest bowl in the set was blue, almost turquoise, then there was the red bowl, and a bit larger green bowl. The yellow bowl was the largest bowl in the set. And at our house, that bowl provided the most delicious memories.

The main use of the yellow bowl was as a mixing bowl. Momma would make her oatmeal chocolate chip cookies in that bowl. First, she would mix eggs and sugar. I would stand on the chair beside her, and she would let me break the eggs, careful not to add any eggshells. Then she would add the flour. At last, she would add the oatmeal and chocolate chips. The batter would be really think. Momma would drop the batter by spoonfuls onto a greased cookie sheet and put them in the oven. Soon the kitchen would be filled with the sweet warm scent of baking cookies. While the cookies were baking, Momma would hand me the beaters and I would blissfully lick them clean! She would lay out a brown paper shopping bag on the counter that she had torn open, and then lay the warm cookies from the oven on top to cool. I always managed to steal away a nice warm cookie... mmmmmm.

Every birthday and most picnics saw the big yellow bowl in use again. This was when the bowl was used to mix Momma's chocolate cake. The cake was actually Grandma Lidgard's recipe, and I was told it had been handed down in the family. Again, she would begin by mixing eggs and sugar. Then she would take her measuring cup and make a mixture of Hershey's cocoa powder and warm water, mixing until all of the cocoa powder was absorbed into the water. This was added to the sugar mixture before she added the flour and baking powder. The batter was a lovely chocolate brown, and the cocoa had

had a wonderful chocolaty scent. She would pour the batter into greased and floured cake tins and then place them in the oven. Oh, the heavenly scent of baking chocolate cake…I can smell it just by remembering it! When the cake came out of the oven and had cooled, she would make her special fudge frosting on the stove and then hurriedly frost the cake before the frosting hardened into a sweet, hard fudge. *Oh, how I miss those cakes!* Nobody ever figured out her recipe for the frosting!

For picnics, the big yellow bowl had yet another use. Her potato salad. Now, this potato salad was in demand at family picnics. First, potatoes and eggs were boiled on the stove. When they had been peeled and cooled, Momma would dice them into the bowl and add chopped onion, green pepper, and celery. Mayonnaise, yellow mustard, and vinegar were mixed together to make her salad dressing, which was mixed into the potato and egg mixture – not too wet and not too dry, just creamy.

Now, if the bowl wasn't used for potato salad, it would be used to make baked beans for the picnic. She would always start with canned pork and beans, but then she would "doctor them up." Adding brown sugar, ketsup, and mustard in amounts only she knew, the beans would be stirred together and placed in the oven for an hour. Needless to say, they came out of the oven bubbling with a sweet, tangy aroma that set your stomach growling!

But the very best memory of the big yellow bowl was reserved for its use on Sunday nights. It was on Sunday night when our family would all gather in the living room to watch *The Ed Sullivan Show* on the television. Momma would come out of the kitchen with the yellow bowl brimming over with hot, salty popcorn. We would all dip our hands in and fill our individual bowls with the fluffy warm kernels and settle in to watch the show.. Momma would eat from the big bowl, and as it emptied, I would join her to eat the partly popped kernels left at the bottom of the bowl. Then, with a full tummy, I would run off to bed – completely fulfilled by the popcorn and the warm feeling of love from an evening spent with my Momma, Daddy and Grandma.

My mom's big yellow bowl has been gone for many years now. But, not long ago, my daughter Julie found a big yellow Pyrex bowl for sale on *ebay* and ordered it as a gift for me. It is now proudly sitting in the center of my dining room table, a warm and wonderful memory of my past. But somehow, the bowl has "shrunk." It doesn't seem quite as big as it once did, but I'll bet that popcorn would taste as sweet as it once did!

Dress for Success

When most people think of a Girl Scout, they usually think of a little girl in a brown dress wearing a brown beanie cap. In my lifetime, that was the way Girl Scouting started, and I still remember the feeling of pride I felt the first time I put on my Brownie uniform. My mom had made sure I had a complete uniform – brown dress, beanie with a little Brownie elf embroidered on the front, anklet socks, belt, and even a little plastic pouch to wear on my belt to hold my dues each week. I felt so grown up and special when I put that uniform on. Little did I know as an eight-year-old what that little brown dress would lead to in my lifetime.

Girl Scouting became part of my heart and soul, part of my very being. It gave me experiences as a girl that I never would have had otherwise. Activities like camping, canoeing, hiking, and horseback riding. As I grew in the organization, there were many uniforms and many activities. There was the green dress with long green sleeves that I wore as a Girl Scout. The badges I earned were sewn onto the sleeves. As I outgrew that uniform, my elbows **popped** right out of the sleeves!

Then came junior high school and a dark green skirt with a white blouse. Our badges were now sewn on a dark green sash that we wore over our right shoulder. We had to learn to tie a square knot so we could tie our yellow ties and place our Girl Scout pin right on the knot.

But now, I learned, there were other "uniforms" to wear. There was a camp uniform of dark green Bermuda shorts with our white shirt and tie. But as we started camping in tents, the "uniform" became quite casual – long pants, shirts to fit the season, maybe a sweat shirt, and maybe a jacket.

Times were beginning to change, and so was the Girl Scout uniform. It was fashioned after a woman's military dress uniform. Dark forest green in color, it was a fitted two- piece suit with an "overseas" cap on our heads. How proudly we wore this new uniform in our final year as Girl Scouts. As I graduated from Girl Scouting and high school, I dreamed of a career in Girl Scouting. I thought it would be perfect working with girls and giving back to those girls the fun and pride I had experienced as a girl.

Little did I know that was to be my destiny! After high school, I worked as a camp aide to my younger sister's troop. I helped them practice their camp skills – putting up tents, building a fire, and cooking over a fire – before we went out on their first camping trip. How I enjoyed that camping trip! The girls stole my pillow the first night, and I slept with my clothes rolled up under my head! But we enjoyed the campfire they built, learning new Girl Scout songs, going on a hike, and just being outdoors.

I took a few years off to be a wife and mother. Then in Italy, I volunteered to coach girls earning their Junior Girl Scout badges. I worked with Julie, who lived next door to us, and her troop. Once again, I fell in love with Girl Scouting and couldn't wait until my own daughter Julie became old enough to join Brownies.

It happened earlier than we expected when Julie became a Daisy Girl Scout, a new experimental age group in Girl Scouts that year. I started working with her leader then became her leader. As a Brownie leader, I worked with a troop of twenty very energetic girls and prepared them to move on to new adventures. We worked on Brownie Try-Its – trying new things – new foods, new outdoor adventures such as hikes and camping skills. We took trips, an overnight in the cabins at Camp Low, and a visit to the Birthplace of Juliet Low in Savannah. The girls soon became Junior Girl Scouts and began real outdoor adventures such as camping out in cold weather and in a "nor- easter"! But I was about to embark on a new adventure of my own – I became a Girl Scout Executive staff member – Training Director and Field Director for the Girl Scout Council of Savannah, Georgia. The dream of a career came true.

Now I really learned about Girl Scout uniforms. I learned that adult uniforms were constantly changing. I began wearing a grass green wrap around skirt with a blouse that had Girl Scout trefoils all over it.

Twenty years later I retired wearing a green Girl Scout dress that had a tie belt at the waist and a silk scarf around the neck. Flashback to days gone by?

My executive role changed when we moved to Tampa in 1987 and I became the Program Director for Girl Scouts of Suncoast Council. Now I learned that my uniform would change with every event planned for the girls in our council. Sometimes my uniform was a teeshirt and shorts or slacks, sometimes I wore funny hats and purple robes, and yet at other times I was very proper and wore the official uniform of a Girl Scout adult.

As my uniforms changed over the years, I began to realize that a uniform was as important as the moment I wore it. I could be formally dressed or I could be casually dressed. What was more important was the significance of the organization represented – an organization that stood for pride in self and country, dedication to strong principles and beliefs, and the opportunity to help others. And I learned that no matter which "uniform" I was wearing at the time, I was always dressed for success.

Twist Me and Turn Me...

I've never forgotten the first time I heard those words. It was a brilliant, crisp autumn day. The trees regaled us in their many shades of green, gold, red, and orange. It was the fall of 1954, and I was wearing my brand new Brownie uniform for the very first time. Brownie troop seventeen was at the Girl Scout Lodge in Plymouth, Michigan. The lodge was a large building sitting on a hill overlooking the Rouge River/Hines Park. It was built of river rock and was two stories high. Inside, it glistened with all its highly polished tables of pine logs. In the center was a large fireplace and on that day, there was a round mirror lying on the floor surrounded by flowers.

Mrs. Luelfing and Mrs. Gretzinger, our leaders, stood by the mirror pond, and we formed a circle around them. Each girl's name was called, and, as she stepped forward, our leaders would turn her round and round...*Twist me and turn me and show me the elf, I looked in the pond and saw.. Myself!* Each girl repeated these words and when done speaking, our leader would pin our Brownie pin on – upside down! We had to do a good deed before we could turn it right side up. After the ceremony, attended by our moms, we had cookies and punch. And so began the exciting years of Girl Scouting for me. I spent many Friday nights in that lodge, sleeping in the lofts high above the main floor.

Our troop met at Bird Elementary School which most of us attended. There were a couple of girls who attended Our Lady of Good Counsel School which was only a few blocks up the street. We met each Tuesday after school for one hour. We made crafts – a jewelry box for our moms made from a square plastic sandwich box. We put a picture of ourselves in the center of the top, then glued glitter around it. I still have my mom's sitting on my dresser. Years later, as a leader, I repeated that craft. We went on hikes in the neighborhood and in the school yard. We even got to hike along the creek running beside the school to see what grew along the creek bed. Our leaders made arrangements for us to take roller skating lessons at our local rink. What fun we had whizzing around the rink and learning special moves! In third grade, we even went on trips such as our overnight stay at the Henry Ford Museum and Greenfield Village. This was our first overnight away from the lodge, and we had so much fun in the dorm and then touring Greenfield Village the next day. My friend Chris' grandfather had helped Henry Ford build Greenfield Village and his house was there, along with Ford's first car, Edison's workshop, and the Wright brothers" bicycle shop.

In the spring of each year, we got to sell Girl Scout cookies! There were three kinds of cookies then – Thin Mints, Shortbread, and Sandwich. The cookies sold for twenty-five cents a box. There was a designated Saturday when all the troops in Plymouth could sell the cookies and each troop had a designated storefront for their sale. Our troop usually drew Dunning's Women's Apparel or Stop and Shop grocery as our spot. All up and down the streets, you could see and hear the other troops as we sold our cookies.

Brownie Day Camp was the highlight of the summer. Each morning for a week, we would all meet at the Girl Scout lodge for our opening flag ceremony. Then, in a double file, we would walk down the path and cross the Rouge River by bridge for our day in the park. Each day of camp had a different theme – Backwards Day we all wore our clothes backwards and walked backwards where it was safe; we even got to eat our dessert first. Pilgrim Day we all dressed as pilgrims, made candles and even had turkey for lunch. Hobo Day was always lots of fun – we dressed like hobos and carried our lunch in a bandana tied to a stick, or one year we learned to make hobo stew for lunch - we each added a can of something to the pot. We made lots of crafts at day camp and we took hikes. One of my favorite hikes was a penny hike – we would flip a penny, and if it was heads, we would turn left, and if it was tails, we would turn right as we walked in the park. We learned about the different kinds of moss that we found, we learned about the different kinds of trees and made waxed leaf collections, and we learned about the insects we found. Then, when the day was over, we would hike back up to the lodge for our closing flag ceremony. It was a fun-tastic week.

We became Girl Scouts in fourth grade, and our uniform became a green, long sleeved dress. As we began to earn badges, we would sew them on the sleeves of our uniform, and as we grew, our elbows began to pop through those long sleeves! Our meetings moved uptown to the Methodist church. We continued to sleep over at the Girl Scout lodge, usually on Friday nights. Did I mention tuna noodle casseroles? That's what we had for dinner every sleepover – *I hate tuna noodle casserole and will not eat it!*

Now, we began to venture out even more. Mrs. Luelfing lived on a turkey farm, and we stayed in her backyard in tents. We learned to build fires and to cook simple meals over the fires. Our favorite treat was s'mores – graham cracker sandwiches with a roasted marshmallow and a piece of chocolate. Ummmm. We took hikes in nearby woods at different times of the year and learned how things change with the seasons. We learned homemaking skills – cooking, baking, and simple songs, games, and storytelling for the care of young children. We began to do community service projects. At first we did things for the church where we were meeting, but then we reached out into the community – a clean-up at Kellogg Park, handing out fire safety information. And we sold cookies, but now we could go door to door selling the cookies, and the price had gone up to thirty-five cents a box.

Seventh grade brought more changes to our troop. The first change was our leaders. Mrs. V now led the troop, and again our meeting place changed. We met at Mrs.V's big white house on the corner of Penniman and Evergreen. She had a big back yard as well. Our crafts now revolved around our badges. We learned to sew – she made me re-do the hem of my skirt three times! But, I finally got it right and was even proud to wear my skirt. We learned how to be proper hostesses – what dishes and silver to use, how to set the table properly, and how to plan a menu. We invited our parents to a dinner that we prepared for them. We began to camp out more and even went to Kensington State Park for the first time. Most of us managed to earn our swimming badge at some time in junior high school. Mrs. V was not an outdoor person so, as we grew older and moved into high school, she found Mrs. T, who loved the out-of-doors. We learned first aid and we earned our First Class rank.

As high school dawned, we were ready for bigger and more challenging projects and outdoor activities. Mrs. T was ready for us! At this point, there was only one Senior Girl Scout Troop in town, ours. And, there was only one Boy Scout Troop in town. We maneuvered to go camping at Kensington on the same weekends.

That way we could play pranks on each other such as pulling up tent stakes in the middle of the night! We also combined our campfires and enjoyed s'mores, camp skits, and of course, singing all the campfire songs – we taught them a few and they taught us a few, too. Mrs. T had a tradition when it came to camping – she would get to the camp site, unfold her camp chair, and sit down, holding her coffee pot. Our campsite was not complete until we girls had all the tents up, equipment put in place, fire wood collected, and a fire built with a grate for the coffee pot! Then, our camp activities could begin. We now camped in more campsites and state parks and different kinds of weather.

One of the most fun took place at the Hillside Girl Scout Camp in Ann Arbor. It was built on a hill and the challenge was finding a level place to put your tent! We went there during the winter and camped in the SNOW! We were always warm and toasty inside the tent, but BRRRR! when we had to get out of the tent. But once again, we went on hikes, learned about the sleeping plants and creepy-crawlys that didn't sleep in the winter. We cooked over the campfire and then enjoyed our campfire songs – *Ashgrove, Girl Scouts Together, Kookaberra, Linger, Baby's Boats, and so many more.*

In our senior year we went to a dude ranch in Grayling, Michigan – up north from Plymouth – for our Easter break. We worked as patrols in preparing for the trip – one patrol planned activities, another planned the packing lists and gear we would take. I was on the third patrol – we planned the meals and did the shopping. The weather was still cool and a bit fresh when we arrived at the ranch, but that did not

hamper us. We moved in, took a tour of the facilities, and got started having fun. Now, we learned to ride horses and we took them out every day on different riding trails. The highlight of the trip was a canoeing trip on the AuSable River, at that time, 1964, touted as one of the most beautiful rivers in the United States. We canoed all day, stopping to eat lunch on the shore, and then going on, shooting the rapids and getting wet in the process! A trip none of us will ever forget.

One of the most rewarding activities for me was as a Candy Striper at St. Mary's hospital. We wore a pink and white apron style dress and even had a nurse's hat that matched. I went to the hospital every Sunday for three months and volunteered on the fifth floor surgical ward. Before we could work on the floor, we took classes in first aid, making a proper bed with hospital corners, courtesy for patients and visitors, and a tour of the floor. During my three months, I delivered meals, answered call lights, made sure the patients had fresh water, and ran errands for the nurses. It was truly a learning experience while being rewarding.

Senior year was also time for us each to plan and carry out a service project and also to carry out a community project. Chris and I worked on our community project together. We were both interested in history, specially about Plymouth as our families were part of that history. We started with her Grandfather Strong. He had designed the city seal and been very active in building Plymouth. He told us a lot about its founders – the Starkweathers, the Pennimans, the Hamiltons, Bennetts, Dunnings, and the Allens. He told us about the history of Daisy Air Rifle, and the growth of the city. From there, Chris and I laid out a historical map of Plymouth, one people could follow and learn about our history. We also wrote a history of Plymouth to go with the map.

My senior service project involved Gene Winters, whose family I babysat for through high school. His civic group was sponsoring a statewide bowling tournament in Plymouth. The men and women of his group would be the hosts and help welcoming the visitors to Plymouth. They were mostly young families and needed babysitters for their children while they were working. My project was to set up babysitters from our troop to take care of their children. The scheduling was brutal, but we managed to carry it off, and my project was a success!

The highlight of our senior year was to attend the National Girl Scout Convention which was held in Michigan. Girl Scouts had a very special spokesman at the time, Debbie Reynolds. She was the Pied Piper of Girl Scouts, and she attended the convention with her daughter Carrie, a Brownie. We got to meet Debbie and Carrie, they were so gracious. I've never forgotten.

Our days of Girl Scouting were coming to an end. We held a graduation ceremony in early June. Dressed in our new dark green Girl Scout uniforms and wearing gloves, we held our final flag ceremony. Mrs. V and Mrs. T presented each of us with our graduation certificate, and we served tea to our moms. It was bittersweet as we reminisced about all the fun we had growing up together, camping, campfires, trips, projects, cookies, but most of all the friendships we had shared. Many of us still keep in touch.

Girl Scouting provided me with so many wonderful experiences as a girl. My parents were not out-of-doors people, but Girl Scouts gave me those experiences – camping, horseback riding, canoeing, and hiking. I was an only child until age ten and it gave me friends. One of my all-time memories from Girl Scouts was learning to make lists – shopping lists, packing lists, lists of tasks. Little did I know how much I would use that one skill throughout my lifetime! Girl Scouts provided me with another way to learn, experiences that I could have only dreamed about otherwise. They say if you scratch a Girl Scout she will bleed green – I am that Girl Scout.

****

On my honor

I will try

To serve God and my country

To help people at all times

And

To live by the Girl Scout Law.

Vanities

As a young child. Saturdays had a very specific purpose in our house. Saturdays were for cleaning! And Sandy had her very own list of chores to perform before she could go outside to play.

One of those chores was to dust my parents' bedroom. This was an exciting and alluring task because my Momma had a vanity. You know – a piece of furniture with a big mirror and you could sit down to put on your make-up, jewelry, and perfume. And my Momma's vanity was my favorite place to explore!

Sitting on her vanity stool, I would move all the perfume bottles from one side to the other for dusting. In the process, I would pretend that I was a great Queen primping for my King. As I moved the bottles, I would sniff each one so I could choose the perfect scent. Let's see – there was the sweet alluring scent of White Shoulders, my Momma's signature scent, the playful but striking scent of Tigress, or maybe the flowery scent of Chantilly. The deep blue bottle of Evening in Paris was beautiful and enticing. Oh, yes. And never forget the exotic scent of Taboo.

Scattered among the perfume bottles was Momma's make-up. Face powder, rouge, the creamy shades of pink she used to color her cheeks, and always, a rainbow of lipstick. Back in the 1950s, red lipstick was THE color to wear.

Her jewelry box sat to one side of the vanity, its contents carefully stored in velvety drawers to keep hem untarnished and ready to wear. Rings, earrings, bracelets, and necklaces of all description slept here, ready to be chosen for any occasion. Here you could find the pink shell necklace and earrings sent to her from far away Hawaii and by a young soldier on his way to war. Or maybe you would like to see the necklace and earrings with the Army symbol that exemplified her pride in her soldier husband. More regal were the pieces of costume jewels kept in the box. There was the sparkly blue set that Momma wore to set off her beautiful dark blue lacey dress, or maybe you select the costume diamond set she wore on VERY special occasions. The jewels seemed endless.

There were two matching hobnail milk glass lamps, resting on doilies she had embroidered while her lover was in the Pacific fighting a war. And perched in front of each lamp, among the finery and perfumes, was a plastic sandwich box decorated with silver glitter and the picture of a little girl – Sandy on one side and Susie on the other. Inside was simple cotton batting used as a cushion for her bracelets and pins.

Resting in the center of the vanity were her brushes, combs, and hand mirror. When you held the mirror up, you could see the back of your head to make sure every hair was in place and... you could admire your necklace and jewelry more closely.

I can still see that vanity today and my Momma sitting there getting ready for a special event in her life. She loved her "pretty things" and looking pretty for Daddy and her family. And, we loved her!

Proud to be an American

Maybe it was because our dads had just fought the war of the century, or maybe it was just because I was young and growing up in the Midwest, but the 4th of July seemed so much bigger back then. It was the 1950s, and I did grow up in a small town...

We anticipated the holiday and prepared for it weeks ahead of time. On the playgrounds, we made decorations as our craft project, and we made plans to be in the parade. Our playground units would put together a "theme," and we would plan our costumes and a float – usually a fleet of red wagons decorated with some patriotic theme. There was one time when we made our wagons look like a wagon train and we dressed up like pioneers. During craft time, we made sunbonnets for the girls to wear and planned to wear long skirts. The boys planned to carry their toy rifles and ride their broomstick horses. Another year, we dressed as revolutionary soldiers with tricorn hats, toy drums with red, white and blue stripes, and we fought the Revolutionary War all down Main Street. Other years, we decorated the spokes of our bikes with red, white and blue crepe paper and put a card in the spokes to make a fluttering noise; we rode as a unit. And on the 4th, we would meet at the gathering point and walk together through town.

The carnival would come to town each year a few days before the holiday. They would set up on the big field behind the high school, which was located at the north end of Main Street. The sky would light up with all their bright lights, and the air was filled with the smell of popcorn, cotton candy, and grilling hot dogs! You could hear the music from the rides all over town, and every kid in town would beg mom and dad for the chance to get up there and take part in all the excitement. The rides were usually ten cents a ride. My favorite was always the tilt-a-whirl. I'd slide across the seat and scream as my seat twirled and spun around and around! But then, there was always a ride on the merry-go-round, finding the fanciest horse for my ride, or riding high in the sky on the Ferris Wheel, safe with my Daddy by my side.

Our 4th of July usually started the night before. Uncle Kenny and Aunt Billie would come out from Detroit and spend the night. Early the next morning, Daddy and Uncle Kenny would get up and head for Hines Park, where they would stake out our claim on a picnic table – always near the playground equipment for me. Aunt Betty and Uncle Walt would arrive early from South Lyon, a small town about ten miles away, and we would pack up the car with all the goodies and head for the park for breakfast. The grass would still be wet and the air cool from the night before. Mom and my aunts would get out the frying pans, and soon the air was filled with the sound and smell of sizzling bacon and eggs. Biscuits baked earlier were warmed on the grill and the table set with honey, homemade jams, and butter. We'd all gather around the table and indulge in the glorious goodies set out for our voracious appetites. Afterwards, my uncles and Dad would take me to the playground while Mom and my aunts cleaned up our feast. By 11:00 AM, we were ready to head back into town for the parade.

The parade would wind through downtown Plymouth from south to north, ending at the high school. There was always a band to lead off, the governor of Michigan always came and walked the parade, followed by the mayor. Then came the fire engines with their blaring sirens; the Veterans of Foreign Wars proudly marched in their uniforms with the women's auxiliary nearby. Then came the kids – each playground had a group marching or riding on bikes, Boy Scouts and Girl Scouts, proud in their uniforms. There were floats by some of the churches and civic groups and of course, Miss Plymouth and her court riding on the back of open convertibles. And everywhere you looked, there were American flags and red, white, and blue bunting.

After the parade, we would go back home and it was time to picnic again – this time at home. Fried chicken was usually on the menu and corn on the cob, along with Momma's potato salad and baked beans. Aunt Betty brought her German potato salad, cucumbers in oil and vinegar, and almost always an apple pie. Aunt Billie was the mistress of banana pudding. Iced tea was plentiful and watermelon was always chilled and ready to eat. One of my greatest memories was the laughter around the table as the adults in my life talked and joked.

As the sun began to set, my excitement grew as I pleaded with everyone to "Come on, let's go to the carnival!" We would usually pack up the car with blankets and set off for the high school field. There, I would ride the rides again one last time for the year and then, when darkness fell, I'd climb on the back of Daddy's car and wait in anxious anticipation for the fireworks to start. At last the booms began and the crowd became quiet…waiting…waiting, then a united "awww" as the first burst lit up the sky. For the next half hour, we became a united town, oohing and awing as each beautiful burst lit up the sky. Then, it was over, and I was usually carried into the house and to bed. This glorious day was over.

Those 4th of July celebrations were wonderful, and they lasted for me until I left home in 1967 as the wife of an American soldier. Our celebrations changed then as we were usually far from home and often in another country. However, some things never changed. There was plenty of patriotic music, American flags everywhere we looked, and the red, white, and blue never changed. We always had a picnic or BBQ with family or friends, and at night, there was always a big fireworks display on base. Of course, there were always soldiers by the dozens, and we were always aware of the price they paid time after time and of the sacrifices they were willing to make at a moment's notice.

But now, it doesn't seem quite the same. In our family, we have a family BBQ and we all get together and serve up the delights of the day. The table is full of BBQ'd chicken or ribs, corn on the cob, potato salad, baked beans, and pies and cookies… But the rest seems to be missing. Where are the parades to celebrate our American pride and spirit? Where are the American flags? Where are the red, white, and blue? Yes, there are fireworks at the end of the day, but the displays are not as numerous or in each community, and many of the displays require an entry fee for the best views. Many people, including my family, put up their own fireworks, thanks to a very ambitious nephew. To hear the patriotic music, I watch television at night and the celebrations in major cities such as Washington, DC, Boston, or New York.

Maybe I am just growing older… maybe its nostalgia… or maybe we really need to get back to the basics of celebrating American freedom. But for me, I AM PROUD TO BE AN AMERICAN!

Where Dreams Come True

Growing up in Plymouth, Michigan, in the 1950s had many advantages. There were lots of playgrounds, swimming lessons at the high school each summer, music lessons during the summer, and so much more. My favorite though, was the two movie theaters downtown. I spent many afternoons in one or the other of the theaters, living in the fairytale worlds that they presented.

The Penn Theater was the newer of the two. Its outer façade was white marble. The entrance area had a red carpet and the concession stand where we could buy hard, juicy Jujube's, chewy caramel Milk duds, crunchy Clark Bars, and salty, buttery popcorn. Then, you would enter the dimly lit theater, find your seat and wait for the curtain to roll back and the movie to begin.

The P&A Theater (Penniman and Allen) was the older theater, and it was showing its age. The entrance area was a bit shabby but still had a concession stand where we could buy goodies to eat. There was a balcony where most of the teenagers sat on Saturday

afternoons. One of the biggest differences was the organ that sat off to the right at the front of the theater. We were told that it once was used to accompany the movies as they were shown. But now, it sat silent.

The Penn Theater got most of the "big" movies, the most popular ones, while the P&A had the westerns, the serials, and most of the "scary" movies. That meant that, most of the time, I could be found

81

at the P&A on Saturdays and the Penn on Sunday. But, I spent many wonderful, dreamy afternoons in both theaters.

Unbelievably, the first movie I remember going to was "The Creature from the Black Lagoon." Even more unbelievable is the fact that my Grandma Lidgard is the one who took me to the P&A Theater to see it! I really don't remember much about the movie except that it scared the bejesus out of me as I hid my eyes in Grandma's coat and held very tightly to her! I wish I could ask her now why she took me to see that movie; it was so out of character for her.

My Grandma was responsible for the second movie I remember watching, and this one was at the Penn Theater. It was a huge movie, in color, and I quickly was lost in the movie and the story. The movie was "Gone with the Wind," and to this day, it is my favorite movie. I was totally swept away by the music, carrying me into the story of Rhett Butler and Scarlett O'Hara and the strife of the Civil War. Hoop skirts, plantation homes with their white columns and gentility told a story of romance and chivalry and sent me into a lifetime of searching history and learning the true facts of our American heritage.

"Cinderella" conjures up different memories, though. My friends Nancy and Susan invited me to go with them and I was extremely excited. It would be my first time at the movies with my friends, no adults. We were all bouncing around the back seat of the car while still sitting in the driveway when their dad slammed the door shut on my hand! He took me, screaming and crying, back across the street to my house where my Grandma doctored my hand. Swollen, black and blue, she put ice on it and then cuddled me until I settled down. I never did see "Cinderella" that year.

When I turned eight, my whole world changed. Bonnie moved in two houses down from my house. We became fast friends and with it came a shared love of movies that grew as we grew. Bonnie had an older sister, Janice, who was ten years older than we were. Janice became our "guardian" on the weekends. We only lived eight blocks from town, so we could walk uptown to the theaters. Of course, Bonnie and I had to finish our chores on Saturday before we could go anywhere. But once those chores were completed and we had our allowances in our hands, we were ready for the movies.

Bonnie and I saw all the grand movies with all the big stars of the day. Love stories like "An Affair to Remember," "Tammy and the Bachelor," "Pillow Talk," and "High Society." Comedies that made our sides hurt from laughing, "Some Like It Hot," "Operation Petticoat," and "It's a Mad, Mad World." We were swept away by the soaring

musicals, "South Pacific," "The King and I," and "Carousel," the songs we never forgot and dancing as we left the theater. And then we cried as we watched movies about World War II, "Sands of Iwo Jima," "Battle of the Bulge." And we watched historic epics, "Ben Hur," "Spartacus," "The Vikings," and "Cleopatra."

On our walk home, we would run and skip and sing our favorite songs. In the fall, we would kick up the leaves that crunched beneath our feet, and in the winter, well…there might be a snowball or two. When we reached the gazebo near the Catholic church, we'd take a short break before walking the last four blocks home.

At home, we mailed for pictures of our favorite stars. We taped the pictures on our walls, made scrapbooks, and collected as many as we could. John Wayne, Cary Grant, Clark Gable, Paul Newman, Rock Hudson, Frank Sinatra, Grace Kelly, Debbie Reynolds, Liz Taylor, Doris Day all appeared in our collections. Sometimes we would trade them, and sometimes just dream about them.

As time passed, we became teenagers, and I moved out of the neighborhood. It was more difficult for Bonnie and me to go to movies and, as we made new friends in junior high and high school, we found more movie friends. Our movies changed, too. We lined up around the Penn Theater and then screamed as we watched Elvis Presley in "Love Me Tender" and then we drooled over Frankie Avalon and Annette in their beach blanket movies.

I started dating Dale, but I wasn't allowed to go to movies with him...or so my parents thought. I would tell them I was going to a movie with Bonnie or Chris and then meet Dale at the theater! One night we went to see "Imitation of Life" with Lana Turner. Dale's parents were supposed to pick us up but something happened and they called my parents to pick us up. We were caught. My Dad was driving and he never spoke a word as he drove Dale home. He was still silent on the way to our house BUT when we got into the house,

WOW, he blew his cork! Needless to say, I didn't see any movies for quite a while!

Bonnie and I were reunited as college roommates at Michigan State University in East Lansing, Michigan. And once again, we were going to movies. Most of the time we caught a bus and went into Lansing to see the movies. That's where we first saw "Mary Poppins" and "My Fair Lady." I fell in love with "Mary Poppins" and knew it was the right movie for my little sister Susie. On my next trip to Plymouth, I treated Susie to that movie, and it became a family favorite too.

Soon after leaving college, I became a wife and mother. Movies were no longer a priority in our family budget, but we still managed to see a few along the way. Dale and I went to see "To Sir, With Love" and "Grand Prix" while we were stationed in Germany. We saw a few more as our kids grew and wanted to see movies. That's how we saw all three of the "Star Wars" movies, "The Sound of Music," "Private Benjamin," and "Ferris Beuhler's Day Off," and many, many more.

I told myself that someday I wanted to own my favorite movies. How? I didn't have the foggiest notion. But then, in the 1980s, a new machine arrived. It was called a VCR and you could buy movies and watch them on your television. Well, my day had come and I began buying my favorite movies. At that time, most of the movies had recently been seen in the movie theaters but, as time passed, the VCR became DVD discs and they began reviving the old movies, my favorites from the past as well as old television shows.

My collection grew with oldies like "The Quiet Man," "An Affair to Remember," "Bridge on the River Kwai,""The Godfather", "The King and I," and the "Sound of Music." But now there were new actors and new movies to provide new thrills, new songs and new dreams. Movies like "Big," "You've Got Mail," "Titanic," "Runaway Bride," "Pretty Woman," and "Star Wars." New stars emerged like Tom Hanks, Harrison Ford, Brad Pitt, George Clooney, Matt

Damon, Julia Roberts, Sally Fields, Patty Duke, Helen Mirren, and many others. My collection is very eclectic, and I am constantly looking for old favorites to add.

I still love going to the movies. Bonnie and I don't get together as much (she is in Michigan and I am here in Florida) but when we are together, we try to go to a movie. I will always love watching movies; they take me away to places I would never go and lose me in their fairy tale stories. They make me laugh, they make me cry, and they make my world a better place to live.

I Have a Sister!

For ten long years I had been an only child – playing by myself on rainy days or playing with Grandma, telling my secrets to the wind, and sharing my toys with my imaginary friends. Now, finally my prayers were to be answered. It was May 23, 1956, and Momma was going to have a baby! Oh, how I had been waiting for nine long months for this day to arrive.

I woke up about six that morning because there seemed to be a lot of noise in the house. Grandma was out of bed too. What was going on? I ran out into the hall where all the hullabaloo was coming from. There was Daddy, carrying Momma's little suitcase, and Grandma was in the kitchen making coffee. Momma came out of the bedroom and gave me a BIG hug. "I'm leaving for the hospital to have our baby," she said. "Be a good girl and do what Grandma tells you while I am gone." "I will, I will," I answered excitedly.

Then, she was gone. I asked Grandma if I could stay home from school, but she said no. "Don't you want to go to the zoo with your class today?" she asked me. Well, sure, what ten year old doesn't want to go to the zoo! Bonnie and I rode our bikes to school but I was so excited about the baby I could hardly think of anything else.

I enjoyed the zoo and *almost* forgot about the baby. We saw the elephants and zebras, visited the hippos and the funny camels with their humped backs. At lunch, we stopped and watched the monkeys with their funny antics! I bought momma a set of salt and pepper shakers, (she really liked salt and pepper shakers) as a souvenir. Then we got back on the big yellow school buses and went back to school.

We got back to our class room, and Mrs. McKenzie told us to put our heads down on our desks and have quiet time. Our principal,

Mrs. Tanger, came into our room and asked if she could see me in the hallway. I was a little scared as I followed her out into the hallway wondering what had I done wrong? Mrs. Tanger bent down a little and asked me if I knew where my momma was. "She's at the hospital having our baby," I replied. Then Mrs. Tanger said, "Well, while you were at the zoo, your momma had a little girl. You have a little sister!"

I was soooo happy!!! I started giggling and laughing. I had a sister! Mrs. Tanger said I could go home, even though it wasn't time to go home. I grabbed my stuff and went outside, telling the janitor about my baby sister on my way out the door. All the way home I was happy, and I kept shouting to anyone who could hear, "I have a baby sister!" Up the hill on our street I rode, yelling all the way. Grandma said she could hear me coming!

Turns out Susan Kay Fielden, my new little sister, was born at 12:15, while I was eating lunch and watching the monkeys, a fact that would come in handy from time to time when she irritated me, which was never very often.

Daddy came home; he looked really tired. Grandma had dinner ready for him. Then my Uncle Orville and Aunt Doris arrived at the house. Uncle Orville was Momma's brother. Everyone was talking softly and finally daddy sat me on his lap. "Your sister is very sick, and we have to take her to a big hospital in Ann Arbor so special doctors can take care of her," he said. Then, he and my aunt and uncle left to go get my sister. Things were pretty bad for the next three days. I later learned that she was RH negative and had to have a full blood exchange, a brand new procedure back in 1956. But after three days, she began to improve.

Ten days later, it was time to bring Susan Kay home from the hospital, and I didn't have to go to school because I was going to finally get to see my new sister. I couldn't wait as I sat in the back seat of the car, imagining all the fun things we were going to share as sisters. I had to wait downstairs in the waiting room while Daddy went to get Momma and the baby. And then, finally, there they were with a little bundle in Momma's arms, my new little sister!

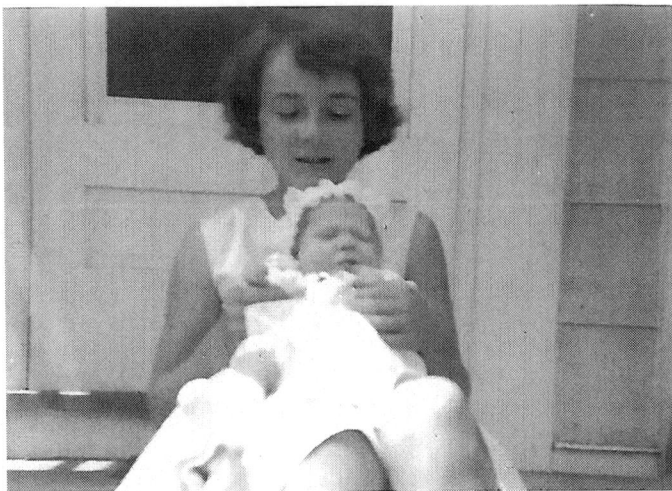

We all got into the car and Daddy placed Susan in my arms. He showed me how to hold her, and then we were on our way home. I just kept looking at her, completely spellbound by her presence. By halfway home, my arms were breaking. I'd never really held a baby before, and I never realized they could be sooo heavy! But, did I complain? NOT on your life! I held that little girl ALL the way home and never said a word.

I had my baby sister. We didn't get to share all those things as children that most sisters share; the ten year gap in our ages made that difficult. But we loved each other and we did play together and shared many things. It has been as adults that we have shared our secrets, our happy times, and our sad times. And it seems that the older we get, the closer we are. I have no idea what I would have done without Susan, and I am forever glad that I didn't have to find out. After all, "I have a sister and her name is Susan Kay."

Prince Charming

I read all the fairy tales so I knew what to expect. One day I could expect the most handsome young prince to come riding up and rescue me from some horrible fate. There was never any doubt in my mind.

But on February 1, 1959, that was the farthest thing from my mind. To begin with, I was still only twelve years old and anxiously awaiting my teen years which were scheduled to start with my thirteenth birthday on Saturday! And Saturday was also the day my family would be moving into a brand new three bedroom house, and I would have my very own bedroom at last!

This was also a very busy week at school. I was joining the Plymouth Junior High School Band. It was semester change, and I was changing my *entire* schedule at school **JUST** to be in band. I started playing the clarinet a year later than all my friends, so Mr. Livingston, the Plymouth Junior High band director, held me back one semester to make up the time through private lessons. And **THEN** he even made me try out for band! But, I did it and now I was in the band. There were new teachers to meet and new friends to make... so many changes.

My new homeroom teacher, Mrs. Larson, sat me next to my girlfriend Chris Cutler. Chris had been my friend since first grade. Mrs. Larson thought it would be easier if I was with my friend. Chris already had a tablemate, so we were a bit crowded at our table.

It turns out that February 1, 1959 **WAS** a *fateful* day. Chris' tablemate was a skinny, freckle faced boy with buck teeth. His name was Dale Cunningham, and right from the start, he was terribly annoying! I sat between Chris and Dale, and in true adolescent boy fashion, he started poking me in the shoulder – *anything to be annoying and get attention.* (Why is it adolescent girls find this annoyance sooo fascinating and exciting?) Meeting Dale was more like meeting an ugly frog!

Well, Dale played the baritone – a big brass instrument that looked like a small tuba – in the band and sat on the opposite side of the band room from the clarinets. It meant that during band he could sit and make faces at me! That was followed by a note writing campaign and then... the gossip began. *"Dale likes Sandy...Sandy likes Dale...Dale wants to go steady...Sandy will say yes..."*

By the time April arrived, things were truly swirling in my life where Dale Cunningham was concerned! April became a turning point for us. The band was scheduled to go to Grand Rapids, Michigan, for the state music festival and competition. All of my girlfriends and all of his boyfriends had paired off to have someone to hang around with at the festival. Everyone it seemed but **US**. So, a week before leaving, Dale asked me to "go steady" and be his girl. I said, "Yes." (Did anyone ever doubt it?) Our fate was sealed. We sat together on the bus ride up and back – I laid my head on his shoulder and pretended to sleep. We held hands and walked around the music festival, and we went to the scheduled basketball game together. The game was the world famous Harlem Globetrotters, the clowns of basketball, but who cared?

Once back at school in Plymouth, we continued to go steady. In May, we attended our first school function together – the Spring Fling. He couldn't dance, and I didn't care. We just kinda shuffled around the dance floor together. There was one sure fact that May – Dale and Sandy were a couple as seventh grade came to an end.

Did I give up so early on Prince Charming? **NO.** I kept looking for him all through high school. Did Prince Charming *ever* arrive? **YES.** Prince Charming did arrive during my senior year in high school. It seems that skinny, freckle faced, buck toothed kid that I had been dating all those years had some dental work done – 4 long years of braces. He also grew ten inches taller and built up some muscle. "**OVERNIGHT**" my frog boyfriend had become my Prince Charming. In his tuxedo, the night of Senior Prom, there was absolutely no sign of the kid from seventh grade, only a shiny, handsome Prince, ready to carry me away to a lifetime of adventure and reality.

FOOTNOTE: Prince Charming and I were married February 11, 1967. It's strange how the years can change a person. Now – three children, nine grandchildren, and one beautiful great-granddaughter and a lifetime of living later – Prince Charming has again changed before my eyes. The beautiful, wavy brown hair has thinned out and turned silver white. The tall slender body has thickened and slowed down, its once graceful movement now slower and more sluggish. Some things never change, though. The teasing, annoying habits of the teenage boy still remain – part of the personality that *never* left adolescence, *never* grew, and *never* changed.

A Lesson Learned

At long last, I was on my way to camp. I had been going to day camps **forever**, but now I was finally going to Girl Scout camp! Cedar Lake Girl Scout Camp was really on Grass Lake, just beyond Chelsea, Michigan. The drive would take us about one and a half hours, depending on traffic. M14, the most direct route, was known as "Bloody Alley" due to all the accidents and because it was so highly traveled as the main east/west highway across Michigan. I got more excited the closer we got to camp.

We finally arrived and I checked in – it took **forever!** First I had to have my physical checked – did I have any allergies? Did I have any physical disabilities? They took my temperature, and they did a physical check of my body for sores, scars, and so on. Whew! This stuff was all on my physical from my doctor! **Finally,** I said good-bye to my parents and set off for my unit and cabin. The camp ranger took all my gear to the unit, and I gathered it all up and moved into my cabin.

There were going to be four of us in the cabin. Jan was already there when I arrived. I didn't know Jan, but we started talking and getting to know each other. Judi was the next one to arrive. Judi was one of my best friends, and we were in the same troop back home. Kathy was the last to arrive. By dinnertime, we were all fast friends as we trekked off down the hill to the dining hall.

That first night as we lay in our beds, we talked late into the night. We found out that Kathy was one of six kids and that her younger sister was also at camp in another unit. Jan had been at camp before, so she told us about some of the counselors and rules. Judi and I shared all about our troop and our adventures over our shared lifetime. Our conversation slowly lulled away, homesick tears were not far away as we listened to the chirp of the crickets and smelled the sweet scent of the pine trees outside our cabin.

Our first full day at camp began early while the dew was still heavy on the grass. My brand new PF flyers got really wet as I walked to the dining hall for breakfast. We all said grace together, and then we listened to announcements from the camp director. She laid out our schedule for the day. The first day was full of *learning and testing* activities. The swim test was high on the list – "dead man's float," tread water for five minutes, swim to the float and back. We knew by the end of camp we would earn our swimming badge and get a Red Cross swimming card – I was working on my advanced swimmer card. There were row boats and canoes as well, but to use any of them you had to take a "tip test." That meant that a counselor went out in the canoe with you and at some point tipped you out of the canoe. It was up to you – fully clothed, by the way – to get the canoe upright and crawl back in! No easy task.

The day at camp usually ended with a campfire and singing. Songs like "Peace," "Ashgrove," "Barges," "Kookaberra," and so many more. Some evenings we had skits with each unit entertaining. When finally the embers began to die in the fire, we would wander back to our units and get ready for bed. And each night, we talked about our families, our friends, and home. Kathy seemed to be the most unhappy of us. She would talk about how much she hated her younger sister who was at camp and how unhappy she was at home. Her mom came under attack often, and she would say how she wished her mom was dead. We didn't understand, but we all tried to talk her out of it, saying we knew she was angry, but she didn't mean what she was saying.

The days passed at camp. We hiked out to the far side of camp with packs on our backs and we camped for three days. One of our counselors was from Oklahoma, and she had the wildest accent, and she told us the wildest stories! Our campfires were full of laughter and fun. We cooked all our meals over the campfire, taking turns as cooks, clean-up, and wood gatherers. One of our favorites was when we learned to make corn pone and pooh butter. The corn pone was really corn fritters and the Pooh butter, well, that was a mixture of honey and butter that tasted great on corn pone! At the end of three days, we hiked back to camp and our beds.

I will forever remember the last night of camp. We had an all camp campfire at the fire circle by the lake. Each unit presented a skit, and the camp counselors entertained us with a skit as well. Laughter rang out over the lake. We sang all of our favorite camp songs and watched as the flames rose into the air. Our bedtime treat was our very favorite treat – ooey, gooey s'mores. Finally, as the embers began to die away, we sang "and as the embers die away, we wish that we could ever stay" as we put our paper wish boats with lighted candles into the lake and silently walked back to our units.

Back in our cabin, we began to pack our duffel bags for the trip home. I couldn't wait to share my adventures with my mom, dad and little sister. We chattered and talked late into the night again, swearing our never-ending friendship with each other – we would write each other and next summer we would come back and request each other as cabin mates. Kathy was the only one who really didn't want to go home; she again talked of her unhappiness and how much she hated her mom. And we still didn't understand.

Morning came, and we all trekked to the dining hall for our final breakfast. The dew burned off quickly in the heat of the day. After breakfast, we formed a single line and walked to "Scout's Own" hill. At a certain point, we were instructed to stop talking and to remain silent until we were told to talk again. We walked silently up the hill and formed a circle around the pine tree at the top. The counselors read short poems about friendship, loyalty, and honesty – the things most honored by Girl Scouting. We sang one last song, Juliette Low's favorite, "Ashgrove." And then we filed silently back down the hill and back to our cabins.

Back at the cabin, we all pitched in to clean the cabin and then to do our unit jobs to make sure we left the unit spic and span for the next group of campers. The counselors came around and checked each cabin before we were allowed to go back to the dining hall to await our parents. It was hard saying goodbye to all our new friends and tears were shed as we hugged good-bye.

I know I chattered all the way home about my camp adventures. Traffic was really slow and backed up forever, so I had lots of time to talk. On the news that night we learned that there had been a really bad accident on M14 that had caused the terrible back-up. A tire had blown off a car and gone through the windshield of the car behind it. That car had been carrying a family, and the parents in the front seat had been killed as well as the baby sitting on his mother's lap. The two children in the back seat had also died. There was only one survivor, one of the daughters, but she was in critical condition at the

University of Michigan hospital in Ann Arbor. We all felt terrible for that family.

The *Detroit Free Press* had more information the next morning about the accident and, as I read the name of the family involved, my heart stopped beating. The lone survivor of the accident was my cabin mate – Kathy. She had lost her entire family in the blink of an eye in a very horrific manner. Her words at camp came back to me of how she hated her mother and wished she were dead and how she hated home.

I never spoke to Kathy again, nor did I write. There was never an address where I could write to her and, at thirteen, I didn't know what words to say to her. But I never forgot those ten days at camp, not the good times and not Kathy's words at night. As I grew older, became a parent, a Girl Scout leader and professional Girl Scout, and then a grandmother, my heart would cringe when I would hear a child say angry words about a parent. Sometimes I shared my story, other times I only admonished, but I always made sure I cautioned others that sometimes our words become reality and we should always think before we speak. It was a lesson I learned at Girl Scout camp.

Easter Break 1960

"Easter break! Yipeeee! A whole week without homework!" I thought as I jumped out of bed the morning after Easter. I was in eighth grade, and I really didn't like doing homework all the time. But, now I was free for the whole week. Mom had gotten me up before she left for work. Grandma wasn't feeling well and had a doctor's appointment that morning; Uncle Bob and Aunt Lucille were coming to get her. That left just Susie, age three, and me for the day.

I was out in the kitchen when I heard a very faint "Help! Sandy, I need help!" coming from my grandma's bedroom. She probably needed help getting dressed, I thought as I went back to her room. There was no way that I was prepared for what came next. Grandma was lying in bed, grimacing and holding her chest. I could tell she was in great pain, and I suspected she was having a heart-attack. Quickly, I moved her back from the edge of the bed. I put two of her pillows under her head to raise it up and then sent Susie to get the two pillows off our bed. These two pillows I put under her feet to raise them up us well, and then I placed a chair in front of the bed.

With Grandma safe, I ran to the kitchen and called my dad's store. Mom hadn't gotten there yet, but Daddy told me to call the ambulance while he called my aunt and uncle. He also said he would send Momma home as soon as she reached the store. I hung up the phone and then called for an ambulance. Having that accomplished, I went back to sit with Grandma. Susie went and got her clothes to wear, and I helped her get dressed, then sent her down to Joan's, our neighbor. I wrote a note for Joan so she would watch Susie for me.

Now, I sat with Grandma, holding her hand and talking softly to her as we waited for the ambulance. The ambulance arrived first, and the attendants came back to the bedroom to take care of Grandma.

Uncle Bob and Aunt Lucille arrived next. Uncle Bob was my mom's brother, and they lived in Plymouth, too. Aunt Lucille shooed me out of the bedroom and out of the way. She always thought children were in the way. Momma arrived as the ambulance was leaving – I think she must have broken every speed limit getting back to the house. They all followed the ambulance to the hospital.

Grandma had suffered a major heart attack, and she would never be coming back to live at our house. It was a sad time for all of us as Momma looked for a nursing home for Grandma. Momma was the youngest of her brothers' and sister but she was grandma's guardian. Grandma had lived with us since Grandpa died in December 1945, before I was born.

The men on the ambulance told me I had done a good job of caring for Grandma while I waited for them. Momma thought I had done everything possible to help Grandma. And me, I thanked the Girl Scouts for teaching me first aid and how to respond to emergency situations.

Easter break did not turn out as I had planned. I had been looking forward to spending time with my friends, Bonnie and Chris, maybe even an overnight. I knew I would be watching Susie, but she usually played outside with Ricky, a neighbor, under the ever watchful eye of his mother, Joan. Those things did not happen during Easter break, though. Susie did play outside with Ricky, but I was more involved, making sure she was safe and playing games with both Susie and Ricky. Momma was gone more than she had planned while she looked into different nursing homes, visited Grandma at the hospital, and helped my dad at the store. My time was used answering phone calls from my aunts and uncles, reading, and listening to music while I watched Susie.

Grandma would live two more years before passing away. She was at West Trail Nursing Home in Plymouth, and we could all go see her. The nursing home even let us have a family reunion there so we could include Grandma, our matriarch. It was quite a happening as Grandma had eight children, 32 grandchildren, and a bunch of greatgrandchildren. Not all attended, of course, but we came out in large numbers for her last reunion with us, and we all enjoyed every minute.

Finances of a Teenager

It was the summer between seventh and eighth grades when a nice looking young man rang our door bell asking for me! He introduced himself as Gene Winters. "I went to school at Michigan State with your cousin Dean," he said. "We just moved into the neighborhood over on Shadywood Drive, and I was looking for a babysitter. Dean recommended I get in touch with you. We have two children; Sherry is eighteen months old, and Tom is three. Would you be interested?" Would I! And so started five years of steady employment and excitement.

Gene and Peggy were very involved in civic clubs in Plymouth. He also worked for a major food market chain and was a young executive on his way up the corporate ladder. These two things combined for a very busy social schedule that kept Sandy quite busy every weekend through my senior year. The children were really nice kids, and we played outside in the summer, played games, read stories, and watched television at other times. I learned how to cook simple meals for young children and shared many meals with them. Sometimes they were already in bed when I arrived.

That was the easy part! Because Gene and Peggy were so active in the community, they were usually involved with the Fall Festival, Fourth of July festivities, bonfires at the Elks Club, and anything else that took place in Plymouth. One of their community groups sponsored the Fish Fry on Friday night at the Fall Festival. I was in charge of French fries! They had a shuttle going between the park and their home where I was pre-frying the french fries while watching two little ones! For sure, I learned about multitasking at a very young age! It seemed there was always something exciting going on, and I was usually part of it in some way.

FIELDEN!!!!!!

Have you ever met a person who so incenses and aggravates you that you think you will lose your mind? A person who rides your behind every day of your life and, somewhere along the way, manages to worm their way into your consciousness so much that they actually manage to bring out the best in you and make themselves a most respected person in your life? Well...I have.

I started playing clarinet the summer after sixth grade. My instructor was Mr. James R. Griffith. He was the director of the Plymouth High School Band. He quite often made his band students mad! By the end of the summer, he had added me to his growing list of unhappy students. All summer, it was "Fielden! Sit up straight!"; "Fielden! Tighten up your embouchure!"; "Fielden! You are out of tune!" I just couldn't seem to do anything right. On the very last day, he met with each student for an evaluation, and I truly dreaded talking to the man. My evaluation was not a very good one. His words to me would ring in my soul for years to come, "You will never be a clarinet player." I left that evaluation with a heavy heart and an anger that boiled deep in my heart.

Regardless of his crumby evaluation, I met with Mr. Larry Livingston, band director of the Plymouth Junior High Band. Since I had started playing clarinet a year behind everyone else my age, he suggested I not enter band in September but wait until second semester. In the meantime, he would give me private lessons to bring me up to the level of the other players. "Sounds good to me," I replied. And so it began. For the next two years, I took private lessons from Mr. Livingston and played in the junior high band. We had one of the top ranked bands in the state of Michigan and, slowly but surely, I began to move up in the clarinet section until I was sitting in the top five chairs. "Tell me I won't ever play the clarinet, will you!"

Now came the time of my revenge: ninth grade and the Plymouth High School Band! I was ready! *At least I thought I was ready.* The band began school one week early. We began practicing our marching and playing since the band marched for all football games. Mr. Griffith (Griff, as we all called him) did not seem real happy to see me that first day BUT I was determined. He stuck me somewhere in the middle of the last row of the band. *"Okay, I can handle this,"* I said. And I did. By the end of marching band season, I had moved out of the middle of the back row and I was proud of myself.

The next challenge came when we had try-outs for our seats in the concert band. This occurred about a month after school started. Try-outs were held in the school auditorium with each student behind the curtain on stage and Griff sitting in front of the stage. We drew numbers for the order we would play instead of using our names. The day after try-outs, Griff posted the order the numbers would be sitting in for concert band. I honestly think he almost fell off the podium the day we took our concert seats – **I, Sandy Fielden, was sitting in second chair!** *It surprised me, too, but I wasn't about to tell him that!* Well, I didn't sit there for very long, and, really I didn't belong there yet, but I had thrown the first volley and warned him that I would not be deterred!

August 1961 arrived, and the Plymouth High School Band headed for Interlochen, the National Band Camp in Traverse City, Michigan. Only the best bands were invited to attend, and we had finally been invited. The first day at camp was taken up with try-outs and with Griff placing everyone for the marching band formation. **SURPRISE!** Sandy Fielden was right guide on! I was almost speechless! Me – a right guide! Well, I quickly learned that it was not all it was advertised to be. For the remainder of that week and all of marching season, anyone within hearing distance of Griff's megaphone would hear the wonderful words **"FIELDEN! Get your rank in line!"**

Concert season brought more challenges. I was now taking private lessons from Griff, of all people. Every Saturday morning I would go to the school and, for one hour, listen to Griff. Since I was also babysitting my younger sister Susie, she would go with me and sit in the back of the room as I played scales and played the same few bars of music over and over and over... During regular band practice on school days, I would move up and down, changing chairs in the second section of the clarinets (there were three sections altogether). It wasn't unusual to hear the words, "Fielden, you are flat!" or "Fielden, you are behind the beat!"

Sometimes, even I thought I would never be a clarinet player!

We headed for Interlochen again in August of 1962, the beginning of my Junior year in high school. Things seemed to change a bit while we were at camp. For one thing, I was now sitting in the first section – *Surprise! Surprise!* Second, I was again the right guide for the marching band on the field. Something seemed to be changing, but I wasn't quite sure if I could trust the changes at all. The fall marching season went fairly smoothly; I didn't hear **"FIELDEN..."** quite so often. We moved on to concert season, and Griff told me he wanted me to enter the Solo and Ensemble Festival, playing a solo! What on earth? I was still taking private lessons from Griff, so he was my coach for the solo. In February, I nervously went to the festival and lo and behold, I received a ranking of two. Not bad for a first try. I felt like I was proving Griff wrong.

Senior year arrived, and back we went to Interlochen. Now, miraculously, I was a leader. Not only was I still a right guide, but I was instructing the Freshmen and Sophomores how to march properly and in line. I was also sitting in second chair, first chair when I felt like exerting myself. **"FIELDEN"** was still being yelled at, but something was different in its sound. All through these years, Griff had teased me about the time I put into Girl Scouts, but now his daughter was in my troop and the teasing stopped. When it came time for the Girl Scout Convention to take place at the same time as the State Band Festival, he didn't complain. All he asked was that those of us attending the convention arrive at the band festival two hours before our scheduled playing time. And, when I arrived, I found him pacing the floor waiting for me! AND, he handed me his clarinet to play! Yes, I was sitting in the first chair, the one chair I had decided never to occupy. Why, you ask? Because I had heard my name often enough to know better than to sit in first chair and receive that yelling every day! The band received a first, and my solo was pointed out as being exemplary. You guessed it, **I was a clarinet player!**

My Senior year was a difficult year. One of my best friends moved away. Other friends stopped including me in activities. My Dad was drinking heavily and was also having financial problems with his business. All of this affected me and how I related to people and my schoolwork. And that's when I realized that Griff was not the enemy and had never been the enemy. My name was never the only name called out during practices. My private lessons had always been full of encouragement My life had changed, but, at eighteen, I wasn't sure how to handle that, and I was too proud to admit it.

Last year, as I looked back fifty years to those days in high school, I fully realized the impact this man had on my life. He challenged me

110

to be the best I could be. I learned that working hard for a goal was an honorable undertaking. And I learned that the rewards were many – I respected myself and my accomplishments, not only in band but in all aspects of my life. I wish I could find Mr. James R. Griffith. I would like to tell him about the impact he has had on my life and thank him for teaching me to set my goals high and to always strive for the best in myself.

Thank you, Griff!

Here Comes the Band!

The cadence of the drum, the lilt of the flute, the trill of clarinets, and the blare of the brass...*hear it! Hear the music, the tapping of the feet as they come down the street! Hear it!* Excitement, the quickening in the beat of your heart as they come down the street, take the field, or play the "Star Spangled Banner," followed by your school fight song! This was the beat of my life for the four years I attended Plymouth High School.

Mr. Griffith was our band director, we all called him "Griff". He was a graduate of the University of Michigan (U of M) music program, ranked as one of the best music programs and bands in the nation. He was a hard taskmaster, especially during the fall, marching season. Our band was greatly fashioned after that revered U of M college band, which meant a lot of work for all the band members but, in the end, it was worth all of our hard work.

Band always started the month before school started. Griff held a one week band camp at the school. All incoming freshmen were required to attend. During camp, we learned all the basics of marching – the U of M high step, eight steps to five yards, guide to the right, straight lines, stay to the beat of the drums, and memorize your music! The older band members would each take a line of underclassmen and drill them on all of these basics. By the end of band camp, we were marching routines for the first football game.

The last day of band camp my first year, we were fitted for our uniforms. Our uniforms were royal blue with white stripes down the trousers and around the wrist of the jackets. The jackets were double breasted with silver buttons, and at our shoulders was a white satin cape that we wore during

marching season. The cape could also be worn on a blue side where the "P" for Plymouth glistened in white satin. (Of course, we took a lot of teasing about that "P" on our backs!) We wore white shirts with a royal blue tie, and on our feet, we wore black shoes with white spats. A grand uniform for a grand band.

We had to work as a unit, whether on the field or in the concert hall, and as we became that unit each fall, we formed the strong bonds of friendships. Most of our friendships were formed within our class – freshmen, sophomores, juniors, seniors – or within our section of the band, such as clarinets, trumpets, drums and so on. The bonds we formed were strong and many lifelong friendships were formed.

I will never forget my first homecoming parade. We formed the band on Forest Street. The air was cool. The crowd was electric with excitement as we began the cadence and started up Ann Arbor Trail, turning onto Main Street. We played our school fight song as our heels clicked to the beat on the pavement and the crowd sang the fight song and cheered as we passed by! All the way up Main Street to the football field behind the school we marched. I was so tired when we reached the field, but the adrenalin rush kept me moving and my heart pounding to the beat!

During the spring of my freshman year, our school thespians put on a musical – The Mikado. More lessons to learn in the band. Shivers ran down my spine as we played the opening chords of the overture, watching the actors take their places and the action begin. We accompanied the actors during their solos and ensemble songs. It was exciting to see how music and the play worked together to make the magic happen. It was a shining success!

Interlochen Band Camp was a nationally recognized performing arts center. Students attended school during the year, but during the summer it became a band camp. A band could only attend if they were invited, and only top ranked bands were invited. Our invitation came during my freshman year. That meant that our band would go during August, just before school started in September.

Oh, the excitement of getting ready to go to camp! We formed committees to get things done. We sold candy to earn money for camp. I was on the "banner committee." It was our task to paint banners to place on the sides of the buses carrying us to Interlochen. We were to be riding in those glorious limousines otherwise known as school buses! There would be three buses – two carrying the band members and one carrying the instruments and equipment. We were going to be a grand procession.

Plymouth is in the southeast corner of Michigan, while Interlochen is just outside of Traverse City in the northwest corner of the state, on Lake Michigan, about a six hour drive on school buses! We really weren't looking forward to that part. Well, it turned out to be a little longer when the equipment bus overheated and broke down about two hours into our trip. It was fixed quickly though, and we were back on the road. All of those banners we worked so hard on, well, they never made it very far. They tore off in the wind of driving!

We finally pulled into Interlochen – beautiful green pine trees

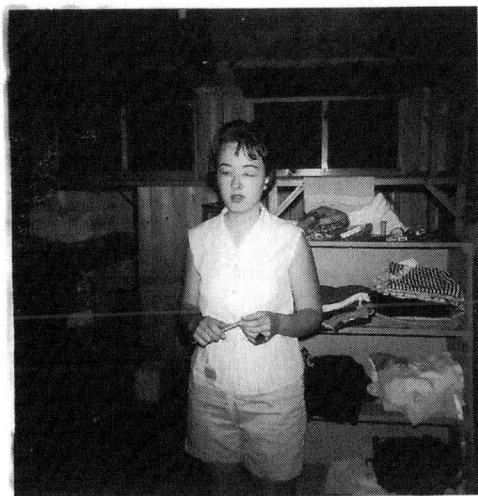

everywhere, sturdily built cabins with a separate room for our chaperones, and indoor facilities, YEAH! We were all in one unit, but a camp road divided the girls' cabins from the boys. Funny thing as I began to unpack, my eyes began itching and watering. Oh no! They began swelling. The chaperones decided I needed to see a nurse and they sent me off in the direction of the nurses' cabin alone! (No Girl Scout buddy system here!) BUT, by the time I got near the nurses' cabin, my eyes were completely swollen shut and I couldn't find the nurse. All I could do was yell for help! And thus was born "Chop Chop," Mr. Griffith's nickname for me all through camp and all three years we attended! My eyes stayed partially swollen all through camp, and later it was determined that I was allergic to those beautiful green pine trees of Northern Michigan.

Interlochen was full of activities. During the morning, we practiced marching followed by concert practice during the heat of the afternoon. There were five bands at camp. In the evening, there were movies, concerts by the different bands, dances and other activities. Our chaperones kept close watch on all of us, but we still managed to break away for

quiet walks on the many paths in camp. We pulled pranks on each other in the cabins – hanging bedding in the rafters, short-sheeting beds, hiding things and of course, there was the flag pole, used mostly by the boys. We worked hard and we played hard and had a great time.

The last day of camp was exhibition day. Each band took the field and put on a marching program. Our program was usually the program we would perform at our first football game. The rivalry between the bands was tremendous – each one wanted to be the best. That first year, we all had a problem, though. We were marching on an open field with the temperature well over ninety degrees. Bandsmen were falling right and left with heat exhaustion, unfortunately, I was one of them. I did make it off the field before I passed out, though! Heat would continue to be a problem for me all of my life.

The last night of camp, we held a concert in the main band shell. Many parents from the bands had been camping in the campgrounds adjacent to Interlochen, and they came for this final concert, as did our chaperones. The highlight of the concert was the final piece, played by all the bands together; "Stars and Stripes" led by Dr. Joseph Maddy, founder of Interlochen National Arts Academy. With hearts beating hard and spirits high, we bid farewell to music camp adventure.

The next day was Saturday and the day we received our reward for all our hard work. The first year, we went to Sleeping Bear Sand Dunes on Lake Michigan. The dunes are huge, but if you can make it to the top, you can walk across them to Lake Michigan. The fun was trying to get to the top, climbing in the soft sand that kept spilling you back down the dune. Our reward the third year was to go into Traverse City and the Cherry Festival. Traverse City is the cherry capital of the state, and each year there is a large festival and a carnival. We

went to the carnival, riding the rides and letting off all the pent up energy we had left.

Interlochen was truly the highlight of our band years, but there was

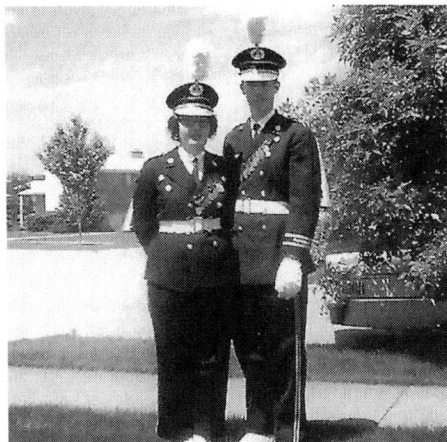

so much more. There were the band festivals where we were judged on our performance; we traveled all over the state for these performances, and, I have to brag, we came home with first division ratings each year. There were also solo and ensemble festivals where individuals played solos or duets, quartets, and sextets formed for judging.

As our years in band came to an end, we had two last performances to make. The Memorial Day Parade took place each year and we led the parade – *hear the drums? The feet on the pavement as they come down the street? The lilt of the flutes? The trill of the clarinets?* In our senior year, this is our last marching performance. The last time we wear our uniforms. Then, suddenly, it is graduation night, and the band sits on the field and plays "Pomp and Circumstance" as we, the Seniors, walk onto the field. The final song of our high school band experience, and we are listening.

My foot still beats to the sound of a spirited march…I still thrill to a fight song… music continues to lift my spirits…guide my emotions… and fill my soul…

You Do Not Go Alone

I have contemplated death and an afterlife many times as I sat beside the bed of a loved one or even thought of my own mortality. In all of my thoughts, there has been one continuing and comforting factor: I will not be alone at the end as I make that final journey from this life into the next.

I was only sixteen when this reality materialized. My beloved grandmother, Nellie Scott Lidgard, lay in a coma in West Trail Nursing Home in Plymouth, Michigan. She had been in the nursing home for more than two years, and I had tried to visit her at least twice a week after school. Now the doctors told us that "her time" was near. It was October 13, 1962, as I walked to the nursing home for probably the last time. But I had a BIG surprise as I entered her room – she was awake, alert, and talking very animatedly. Of course, she was talking to the corner of her room – you know, where the walls meet the ceiling. She was not aware of my presence at first, so I just sat and listened to her conversation. She was saying, "I'm not quite ready yet. I need to tell the children I am leaving," and "I still need to get dinner and finish the laundry," and "You will just have to wait." When I did get her attention, I asked her just who she was talking to. "Your Grandfather. He's right over there waiting to take me home, but I'm just not ready yet." My Grandfather died two months before I was born, and she very rarely talked about him. But today, she said, he was very impatient and it was her time, she didn't need to suffer any longer. I sat with her a little while longer before I walked home. It was my last visit with her; she died three days later, and I knew in my heart that my grandfather had waited there, at the end of her bed, to walk her home to her final rest.

It was many years later when Dale and I sat at the bedside of his mother, Helen Cunningham, that I thought of these things again. She

119

had spent most of the summer of 1995 going back and forth between our house and the Intensive Care Unit at the hospital. Now, she was failing, and we were spending her last days sitting with her. It was August 30, her final day with us. Her bed was slightly elevated, and now and then she spoke with us. However, she spent most of her time that day "flirting" with the end of her bed. She would get a sheepish little grin on her face and then wiggle a couple fingers in greeting. She was talking, as well, but so softly that we could not understand her words. As I watched her, I remembered my grandmother and our final visit. I told Dale, "Your dad is here." He surprised me, "I think so, too." The thought comforted both of us. That night, she slipped quietly away, and we both knew that Dad had walked with her, holding her hand as he always had.

It's been ten years now since I once again experienced this phenomenon. This time it was my closest friend, my momma. My sister Susie and I had been sitting beside her bed at West Trail Nursing Home for three weeks. We knew that her time to leave us was very close. It was Sunday night, and the staff asked if we would like to spend the night with her. We were sitting beside her about midnight when she became very agitated and restless. She began to moan and make little crying sounds. Susie and I tried to comfort her but to no avail. Suddenly, her left arm raised up, and she made a motion as if she were taking hold of a hand. She immediately calmed down and brought her hand back under the covers. I pulled the covers back to make sure her hand was not hanging off the bed, but what I found amazed me. Her hand was lying on the bed, cupped as if she were holding a hand. Susie and I shared a glance at each other and agreed that we both felt much calmer as well. It was at that moment we both realized that our dad had come to be with her, to hold her hand as they went home together.

There was a popular movie a few years ago starring Patrick Swazye and Demi Moore. It was called "Ghost." Near the end of the movie, Patrick's character tells Demi's goodbye as he walks toward a beautiful glowing light. But, in the light, you see figures moving as he walks into the light. I cried during this scene because there, on the screen, was the belief I have held most of my life. When that glorious day arrives that I pass into the next life, I will be greeted by all the souls I have loved so dearly, and we will be together for eternity.

Questions of Faith

Outside the window, the trees were changing colors, putting on their finest reds, golds and oranges. The air was crisp and the smell of autumn filled the air. Inside, my heart was breaking as I sat beside my Grandma Lidgard's bed at west trail Nursing Home in Plymouth. She had been in a coma for several days and we all knew she would not be with us much longer. Grandma had suffered a massive stroke.

It was October 1962 and I was sixteen years old. Grandma had been

my best friend since my birth and I already missed her terribly. She had given me so much including my faith in God and His goodness to all who believed in Him. I had gone to church with her faithfully

each Sunday – taking part in Sunday School, choir and youth groups. When I was ten, I accepted God as my Savior through baptism. And yet, as I sat beside her bed, my soul was in turmoil. Questions began to form ....*how could God make someone suffer so much, someone who loved and believed in Him?* It seemed everything I had learned was now in question.

She passed away on October 17, 1962. The world was embroiled in the Cuban Missile Crisis, holding its breath to see if the United States would strike against the Russian missiles in Cuba. I missed the entire crisis as my family mourned grandma's passing. Our minister was new to our church, Rev. Williams, and he never met her but he gave a beautiful service, likening her death to the life of a butterfly that has now awakened in heaven. It calmed me to hear those words and to visualize her as a beautiful butterfly in God's heaven.

That peace did not last long though. I was very angry – angry at God, not for taking grandma, but for making her suffer for two long years! My childhood faith had been shattered. The kind and loving God I had always believed in no longer existed in my heart. In His place was disbelief and betrayal. *My mind raged against everything I had ever learned in church.* I questioned His being, His love, and the words He had given us in the Bible. God no longer existed in my life.

After several months, I began a series of weekly meetings with Rev. Williams. I no longer attended church nor did I pray. The pastor insisted on starting each session with a prayer, but I did not participate. He was very patient as he explained that the devil was fighting for my soul. Ha! I didn't believe that! Then came his belief that my grandma had suffered for so long as "part of her work here on earth. It was obvious that she was to teach God's love to someone by her suffering." *I didn't believe that either! A loving God would not do that to a loving and devoted follower.* Our meetings went on for a year, actually for three years but not on a weekly basis. My anger subsided but I no longer trusted in the goodness of the Lord.

My life moved away from Plymouth and further away from the church. I continued to follow His teachings, I just did not acknowledge His existence in my life. As my children grew, I began sending them to Sunday School at the Base chapel. I felt they needed "something" in their lives and the knowledge necessary to make their own decisions concerning religion.

In 1987, our family moved to Tampa. Kenny was now grown and on his own, Jason was fast approaching that same place in his life and Julie was entering a period of upheaval in her life. Jason began dating a young woman named Christy who would eventually become his wife. She was attending the First Baptist Church of Lutz and slowly introduced our family into that congregation. I found comfort and familiarity attending church services and a feeling of peace that had been missing in my life. And yet, the nagging questions of my youth remained unanswered.

I made an appointment to meet with Pastor Charles and ask once again about my nagging doubts. Once again I found patience and understanding in Charles. But there was a difference in his responses. He asked me a question I had never considered. He asked if I had ever considered that the devil, not God, had prolonged her suffering – an attempt to steal a worthy soul. *Wow! In all these years I had never considered that possibility. I had thought only to blame God for her suffering.* Wouldn't it be wonderful if questions of faith could be answered so easily?

Pastor Charles had given me something new to think about and to pray about. He had also given me passages to read in the Bible. One more element, Charles had told me that even though I had abandoned the Lord, He had not abandoned me….He had always been there when I needed Him. *I had so much to think about…to pray about.* As I once again began to pray for guidance, my mind wandered back through the years…*the doctors said I could not bear any children, yet I had born three miracles…the doctors said Jason would die within two days but he survived to grow strong and healthy…Dale went to fight a war and came home safe…and I could think of other times when the world seemed dark and forboding but somehow we always made it through.* I began to realize that God had always been there, protecting and comforting. It was I, Sandy, who had strayed and questioned. I realized the time had come for me to fully accept God as my Lord and Savior, to trust in Him only and to follow His teachings.

All of that happened back in the early 1990's. I rejoined the church then and found a peace and understanding that had been missing in my life for a very long time. Since then, all three of my children have accepted the Lord as their Savior through baptism and my grandchildren are following in our footsteps as they become old enough to make their own decision. *I no longer question or doubt His presence in my life, I know beyond all doubt that He is near and through prayer I can take my concerns and love to Him...**ALWAYS.***

The Week We All Grew Up

It's been fifty-four years and yet the week of November 21, 1963, is burned in my memory. It was my senior year in high school. My life at that time was full of college entrance forms, college financial forms, band, football games, pajama parties, and all things teenage and high school. Dale and I had broken up in September, and I was still trying to define myself without him. Of course, I had to see him every day in the band room and every Thursday night when we had band practice.

The night of November 21 was a Thursday, and we had band practice as usual. It was a normal band practice, and nothing seemed out of the ordinary. Dale had to mouth off at me as he had been doing all along. He was dating another girl in the band and, of course, he had to make sure I was aware of every move he made. Joy also played clarinet, and she sat behind me in band, whispering loud enough for me to hear about every little thing they were doing together. She was a junior, and Saturday night was the J-Hop, and I knew every detail about her dress and her plans.

My plans were also set. I was excited about the Suburban Six music festival to be held the next night at Taylor High School. I was getting to miss school all day Friday as we would be at Taylor practicing for the concert. It was for the band, choir, and orchestra, and I had waited all through high school to be chosen for this Suburban Six band. It was for the best of the best. Then, on Saturday night, the night of the J-Hop, my clique of seniors was going to have a pajama party at Chris' house, two houses from the high school and on Main Street. We had some scurrilous plans for that night, too!

Everything seemed perfectly normal and peaceful in my world as I left band practice and headed home. But, as I was driving along, it seemed I had a car behind me, following me. That made me a little nervous as I pulled into my subdivision. My plan was to pull into my driveway and run for the front door screaming. The car pulled up behind me in the driveway and then… I recognized the other car and its driver. It was Dale.

He jumped out of the car and blocked my way to the door. He said that he just wanted to talk. So, there we stood, outside, leaning against my car, talking for what seemed like hours. It wasn't that long, but it was about an hour. He apologized, he told me what a big mistake it had been to break up with me. Couldn't we please makeup and get back together?

I asked, "What about Joy? Aren't you going to the J-Hop on Saturday?"

"Yes, but she is really just a friend. I don't like her in the same way as I do you." Well, sucker girl that I was, I believed him and took him at his word.

"What are you going to do about Joy?" I asked. "What about Saturday night?"

"It's her J-Hop, and I can't disappoint her. I'll still have to take her, but I'll tell her after the dance. I'll get my class ring back and give it back to you on Monday. Will that work?" he asked.

Well, that was our plan as we headed into the weekend. But, our plans were about to be interrupted by the worst event of the century and of our lives.

November 22, 1963, dawned cold and dreary. There was a slight drizzle, and freezing rain was forecast. But for me, it was an exciting day. Tonight was the Suburban Six Music Festival. I would be sitting first chair clarinet, the most coveted position. I had worked hard for this honor, and I was looking forward to the concert.

At 9:00 AM we boarded the buses to travel to Trenton, Michigan, where we were to spend the day in rehearsal for the evening's concert. The bus was full of chattering band members, all of us glad to be out of classes for the day; talk centered around the junior prom the next night, our latest chemistry test, and, of course, tonight's concert. By 11:00 AM, we were busy practicing and getting to know the band members from the high schools. Trenton High School was a brand new high school that wasn't in use yet. Only the office staff was in the school, getting ready for the opening on December 1. At noon we took a forty-five minute break for lunch.

After lunch, we resumed rehearsal with the music from the Broadway show "Oklahoma." The notes to the piece floated in the air as we followed the direction of the band director from Trenton. At this point, my own band director entered the room looking very somber. He whispered something to the director on the podium, and then he took the podium. We sat in stunned silence as he announced that President John F. Kennedy had been assassinated. Then, we burst into nervous tears, disbelief, and shock. How could this have happened to our president? What had happened? Was anyone else hurt? Was our country under attack?

While all of these questions raced through our minds, the band directors were busy trying to make decisions and keep us calm. They had us continue practicing, but it became apparent that we were too upset to accomplish anything. Finally, they released us from rehearsal and let us put our instruments away. We sat in groups and talked quietly while we waited for a decision. About 3:30, the directors came in and announced that the concert had been canceled and we would all be going home within the hour.

There was only one radio in the school; as we boarded the buses, we had a lot of rumors swirling in our heads. As far as we knew, Jackie had been shot, Lyndon Johnson had been killed, and so had the governor of Texas. The bus ride home was long and sad. The freezing rain that had been predicted made the roads hazardous and the trip longer.

We finally arrived at the high school, to be met by our parents, who were in as much a state of shock as we were. It was good to be home – to be with my family in familiar and friendly surroundings. Outside my home, the world was swirling, nothing seemed safe. The world had turned upside down. The news wasn't as bad as the rumors we heard. Jackie wasn't hurt, Johnson was alive and had been sworn in as our new president, and the governor of Texas was still alive. It helped, but it did not take away the pain of Kennedy's death.

Little did we know what the weekend had in store for us. With my mom and dad by my side, we sat glued to the television almost all weekend. It seemed the world had come to a halt – major events were canceled, the concert was canceled and never rescheduled, and the only thing on television was stories about "Camelot," the Kennedys, and all the events surrounding his death and his funeral. But, our J-Hop was to go on as planned.

That Friday night, Dale and I talked on the phone for an hour, something never allowed before. The relationship that was repairing itself found us consoling each other as never before. I think the assassination brought us closer together than we had ever been.

Dale kept his date with Joy for the J-Hop on Saturday night. And we kept our date with the pajama party. We cried, we watched the television and the events unfolding in our nation. And then we did something totally out of character for our group – we snuck out of the house, toilet paper in hand, and we went "TP'ing" in town. We would hide in the bushes whenever we saw a police car or any car! The houses we selected were people we knew such as members of the football team, band members, and Joy's house! We'd throw the toilet paper roll into the air so that it would catch on the limbs of the trees and shrubs. We laughed and giggled and, for those couple of hours, we were teenagers without a care in the world. We set reality aside.

On Sunday morning, I went to church with my mom. Our pastor

talked about the assassination. We prayed for our country, the slain president and his family, and we prayed for the safety of our new president. When we got back home, we turned on the television, only to learn and watch the killing of Lee Harvey Oswald. To watch a second murder on television was unthinkable and horrifying.

School was canceled on Monday so we could be home and watch the funeral. Dignitaries from all over the world came to pay homage to our slain president. Jackie dressed completely in black with a heavy black veil. Caroline and John, so young and so unknowing. The dirge, the horses' hooves on the pavement, the muffled drum beat, the throngs of silent onlookers all along the funeral route, and then the salute from little John. We cried non-stop for hours. And the images remained – not just for a day or a week, but for a lifetime. The common question for our generation became, "Where were you when you learned about Kennedy's assassination?"

November 22, 1963, was the day our nation lost its innocence. The world changed over- night and became a place full of danger. Our country was vulnerable and the questions we asked went unanswered. We had witnessed history firsthand. Overnight, we had grown up and taken on the responsibilities our young president had challenged us with in

his inaugural address. It was a time for growing, for learning, and it was the beginning of becoming adults.

~~~~~

Let the word go forth from this time and place, to friend and foe alike, that the torch has been passed to a new generation of Americans, born in this century, tempered by war, disciplined by a hard and bitter peace, proud of our ancient heritage...

Let every nation know, whether it wishes us well or ill, that we shall pay any price, bear any burden, meet any hardship, support any friend, oppose any foe to assure the survival and the success of Liberty.

And so, my fellow Americans: ask not what your country can do for you – ask what you can do for your country.

Excerpts from the inaugural address of President John F. Kennedy, January 20, 1961

Class of '64

September 1963 saw our class report to Plymouth High School (PHS) for our final year. We were a very special class, we were told. First, there were three hundred-forty-nine of us, the largest senior class ever at PHS. Second, we were the first class of baby boomers – born in 1946; most of our fathers fought in World War II. Plymouth had built two new elementary schools when we had started kindergarten! And third, we were considered to be the last class of "good kids" – they were already anticipating problems with the larger classes that would follow us, thing such as drugs. Our class' biggest problems were basically smoking and drinking beer.

We were all excited as we started the new school year. After all, it was our final year. I was busy that fall filling out college applications and financial forms. There were so many forms! I applied to Michigan State University, the University of Tennessee, and Arizona State

University. Michigan State was my first choice, but I would have been happy just being accepted someplace.

Dale and I were still going steady, and I was looking forward to all the things we would be doing. Well, that idea didn't last long! Two weeks into the school year, we had a huge fight that culminated on the football field during our Thursday night band practice. I had worn Dale's class ring since we received them as Juniors, but that night I was sooo mad at him that I threw it at him on the field! "Griff" wasn't very happy with me, because we had to take time to look for the ring in the grass! Oh, well, I made my point!

Soon after breaking up, Dale started dating one of our majorettes; she was a Junior. I started dating Henry, also a Senior. Dating Henry turned out to be one of the best parts of my Senior year! We always had a great time together. Homecoming was in October, our class unfurled our class flag at halftime – Mickey Mouse – and we all stood and sang the "Mickey Mouse Club" theme song. After the game, we all went to the homecoming dance in the school gym. I was still in my band uniform, but who cared; Henry and I danced the night away.

Halloween soon followed. Henry and I dressed as two hoboes. We burned cork and then rubbed it on our faces and arms. We blacked out our teeth by chewing Black Jack gum and sticking it on our teeth. Dressed in all our "finery," we went to our youth fellowship Halloween party at the Methodist church. No one could guess who we were, and we won the prize for best dressed!

Henry's birthday was in early November, and his parents gave him a fantastic party. It was a city-wide scavenger game! We were divided up into groups of four per car. Then we went around town, collecting the items on our list – a glass from A&W, a napkin from Daly's drive-in, and so on. Henry was afraid we were winning, so on our way back to his house, he threw the car keys out the window! It was no fun trying to find the keys on a country road, but we were eventually successful! Back at his house, we enjoyed hot cider, popcorn balls, birthday cake, and ice cream. Henry could only go out with a girl three times, then he had to take a break and see other girls for a while. We made plans to go out again, after he went out with a close friend.

November brought us some very cold, snowy, and wet weather. Our football team was undefeated, which meant we played extra games for the title. One of those Friday night games was extremely cold, temperature in the teens, and snowy and wet. The football team churned up the field as they played, and at halftime, the band had to march in muddy, slippery muck on the field. I always marched onto the field behind a tuba player, and that night, I was afraid he was going to fall backward onto me! Our feet were cold and muddy after our halftime show. Some of the kids had heavy parkas to keep them warm, others had blankets. It was all worth it, though. We won the game, and we were the division champs!

In the meantime, Dale reappeared in my life! He followed me home from band practice on Thursday night, November 21. It seemed that he wanted us to go steady again. He was sorry we had broken up. Only thing was, he was taking Joy to the J-Hop on Saturday night. But we could start going steady again on Monday. Well, I fell for it and agreed!

Then came the horrific events of November 22, 1963, the assassination of President John F. Kennedy (another story). It was the event that would forever mark our class and change our world. Dale and I spent the weekend talking on the phone while we kept up with the events taking place on television. We had Monday off school for the funeral, but on

Tuesday morning, Dale met me at his locker and gave me his class ring. We never fought again that year.

In January, our class decided it was time for our class prank. It seemed we all needed to go to the library. As we left, we took an armload of books with us and hid them in our lockers! We managed to come very close to emptying the library of its books! Needless to say, the librarian wasn't very happy with us.

January was a busy month in other ways as well. We received our class rankings. With a 3.87 grade average, I ranked number ten in the class! That was both a surprise and a relief. Next came college acceptance replies. I had been accepted to all three of the colleges I had applied to. Naturally, I accepted MSU, and so did my best friend Bonnie. We agreed then and there to be roommates the next year.

I was also practicing for the state solo and ensembles, both for band and choir. I was singing a solo for the choral festival. Every afternoon after school, I would go over to my friend Chris' house to practice. Her mother was my accompanist. I was as comfortable at her house as I was at mine. She only lived one house away from the school, and I had been eating lunch there every day for four years. Her dad was a lawyer, and he was always challenging us to "think" at lunchtime. He was so much fun and taught us so much. I received a "two" on my solo at the festival.

I was also playing a clarinet solo for the band festival. "Griff" was helping me, and I was meeting him every Saturday at the school to practice. Because I always took care of my sister, Susie, on Saturdays, she would go with me and sit quietly reading or playing games while I practiced. Well, I also received a "two" on my clarinet solo, but only because I had my music on my stand. I hadn't used my music but put it there "just in case." My judge was the clarinet director at UofM School of Music. He stood up at the end of my solo and offered me a scholarship to UofM! I almost fell over. Needless to say, I didn't accept it, but it was a real honor.

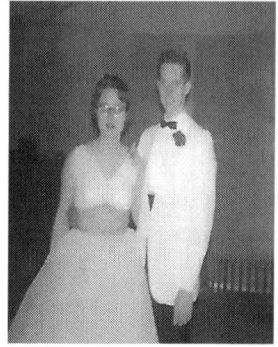

Senior Prom was our next major event. Dale and I doubled with our friends Maggie and Lynn. My dress was everything I had ever dreamed it would be. It was a floor length gown with a hoop underneath. The cloth was white dotted swiss with a pink waist that tied in a bow in the back and then flowed to the floor as well. I felt like I was a princess. Dale arrived in a shiny white tuxedo with a corsage of pink baby roses. He was definitely my Prince Charming that night. We all went to dinner at the Dearborn Inn in Dearborn, Michigan. It was a very posh restaurant, and we were the only people in formal dress. Well, Maggie and I got the giggles, and we couldn't stop! We giggled all through dinner! Dale and Lynn were not very happy with us, but we had fun.

On May 31, I skipped school for the very first time. Dale and I, with several of our friends, took the day off to go to graduation at UofM. President Lyndon Johnson was delivering the commencement address. That was the only time I ever heard a president speak in person until I heard President Obama speak in 2009. The band was playing for the opening of the new city hall that afternoon, and we were a little late getting back but still in time to play.

Suddenly, it was June 11, 1964. As Seniors, we walked on to the football field to the strains of "Pomp and Circumstance," played by the high school band. It seemed strange not being with the band; change was happening. We sat on the field listening to the speeches; I have no idea what was said. My thoughts roamed as I thought back to hayrides, football games, dances, and all the fun of high school. I knew I would probably never see the kids in my class again or share experiences with them. Then, it was my turn to walk across the stage and receive my diploma. High school was over. We flipped our tassels and walked proudly off the field.

New Beginnings

September 14, 1964, had finally arrived. The dream I had worked for so long and so hard was finally coming true. Today, I was officially a student at Michigan State University. Even the weather was happy for me. The sky was a beautiful clear blue, and the trees were beginning to show off their fall finery. It couldn't be a more perfect day...

Well, maybe it could have been a little better. I had always known that I wanted to go to college to become a teacher. That's why I had spent four years of high school studying hard, and it had paid off. I had a full scholarship to Michigan State. During the summer, I had worked at my Dad's grocery store, the Grandway Market, and saved the money to pay for books and other supplies. What I hadn't planned for was my Dad's struggle to keep the store open. I wasn't really aware of the depth of the problem on September 14, but I knew my Dad was worried.

Our "good" car, a Pontiac, was not running that morning. That meant we had to pack all my school gear into the old 1959 Rambler that was used to deliver groceries at the store. Dad didn't want me to be seen at school in **that** car, so Momma had made arrangements with her sister, Auntie Arvella, for us to stop at her house and change cars. Auntie Arvella lived about half way between our house in Plymouth, Michigan, and East Lansing, home of the university. With all my gear moved to the new car, I rode blissfully on to school and the fulfillment of my dream.

Fall semester was a busy time. I lived on "new" campus, meaning our dorms were the farthest from the classroom buildings. Newer buildings were being built but weren't ready for students yet.

Learning how to get around campus and getting used to classes of 50 to 300 students alone was a daunting task! But there were other things to adjust to as well, like getting yourself up in the morning, making it to the cafeteria for meals before it closed, and sharing the shower with four other people! **And** there were all kinds of new activities to try out! The football stadium was right across the street from our dorm, and Michigan State was nationally ranked as well as being #1 in the Big Ten conference that year. There was no way that I could miss those games! So, I joined the card section – we sat in the corner of the stadium with large cards that spelled out words and cheers during the games. There were hootenannies to attend (you remember, "sing-alongs" with political attitude?), concerts to attend, and, of course, there was studying to do as well. It was easy to get home on weekends. Bonnie and I, my best friend and room-mate, shared rides back and forth or we took the train. We went home

about every three weeks. Things really didn't seem any different at home. I didn't know that my parents had a pact not to talk about the store and money while I was

home. But as Christmas approached, I sensed a different atmosphere when I visited... furtive looks between my parents, long pauses during conversations, and an overall feeling of uneasiness. Christmas break arrived, and I came home for three weeks.

The week before Christmas was busy with baking, attending my younger sister's school activities, and last minute shopping. Momma and Daddy made Christmas the happy season it had always been. I was still pretty much in the dark as to the cloud that was building over my head.

When Christmas was over, my parents sat me down to discuss some changes that we needed to be made. The store was failing completely. It wasn't the store itself. Actually, it was the landlord putting the building up for sale without my Dad's knowledge. But, because of that, my Dad was going to have to close the store, and he was deeply in debt. Bankruptcy was his only answer, and that had dire consequences for me… I would have to leave school at the end of March. There was no money to pay my dorm fees and living expenses.

However, I was good to go for another semester, so I went back in January under a heavy cloud. My grades slipped, and for the first time ever, I was threatened with academic probation. Winter term wasn't as much fun as fall term, and I struggled every day. Michigan State was on a trimester system (three sessions instead of two) at that time, so when March came, I packed up my gear and moved home. It was one of the lowest moments in my life.

By summer, we had moved out of our house and into an apartment. I was sharing a room with my eight-year-old sister Susie, and I had a job working in a factory. But, I was saving every cent I could get, and I applied to the community college. When August arrived, I was once again in school, and I had gotten a better job working as a phone operator at a local hospital, St. Mary's, in Livonia. My dad had two jobs – working full time for Kroger as a head meat cutter and part time working as a meat cutter for a friend. My Mom was working as a clerk at Dunning's, a local women's clothing store, and selling Bee-Line clothes on the side. Bee-Line sold clothes on the home party plan. Susie and I got to model the clothes for Momma.

Those years were a struggle for all of us. But somehow, we all seemed to become more determined and closer as a family. I lived at home for a year and a half before I moved out and on with my life. I didn't graduate from college until 1993, when I graduated from Eckerd College in St, Petersburg, Florida. My parents were in the audience that night as I graduated with honors – and my Dad was beaming. Their lives had greatly improved in the ensuing years. They never actually filed for bankruptcy – Daddy's creditors respected him too much to force him into that position. In the end, he had paid them all back, every penny. He retired from Kroger in 1982. Mom and Dad lived comfortably in retirement for almost twenty years before he passed away.

I learned so much from those years. Momma and Daddy were a team, working together to give their daughters the best life they could. We were never "rich" financially but we never wanted for anything, and we made the best of what we did have. The important thing was that we had each other, and together we could achieve anything.

Planes, Boston, Dale, Change.......

The Fourth of July weekend was a four-day weekend in 1965, and I had been anticipating it for weeks. My job at the Burroughs factory had been a hot and greasy job. Hired as a file clerk, I never dreamed that meant walking through the hot plant twice a day collecting the greasy parts cards for the adding machines and taking them back upstairs to be filed in greasy bins. I was going to escape this weekend and fly to Boston to spend an exciting weekend with Dale! There was only one drawback, Dale's parents would be there to "chaperone" our weekend.

Dale and I had set our wedding date for the Labor Day weekend. The invitations were addressed and ready to go, I had my dress, my shower date had been set, and now we'd be able to complete our plans. He was stationed at Fort Devens, just outside of Boston, and we hadn't seen each other since March. Now was our chance to just enjoy our time together as we looked forward to our future.

I had never flown before, so my stomach was churning as I boarded the American Airlines plane. But, here I was… *traveling by myself, flying!* My mind was racing as the engines wound their way to full speed and the wheels lifted from the runway…*would I make it to Boston, did I have a future or would this plane fall out of the sky, would Dale really be there to meet me?* The captain came on the speaker and told us to prepare for our final landing as we approached Logan Airport… *we were already there, two hours went quickly,* NO ONE WARNED ME THAT WE WERE LANDING OVER WATER, OH, LORD, HELP ME! We landed, wow, we actually landed! And there was Dale, waiting for me, and I was in his arms, and the world was perfect again.

Of course, his parents were there, standing right behind him, but we could handle that. They had always been there... Interlochen, band festivals, picnics, everywhere we went. I already had memories of good times with them, and I didn't doubt that we would enjoy this trip as well... *I just hoped they would give us some time together, alone.*

The weekend was a busy one, filled with all the sights of Massachusetts. During the weekend, we visited Plymouth Rock, the Plymouth Colony – if I had only known then what I know now about our ancestors – Lexington, Concord, and Old North Church. We went out to a big amusement park at Revere Beach, and finally we were alone to have fun. I'll never forget that park and its HUGE ROLLER COASTER! Dale had to ride it. I boarded it with great trepidation... *I was not a roller coaster fan!* But here I was, Dale's strong arm around me, holding me tight – then I was screaming, holding on to Dale with all my might, **then my glasses flew off! Away they flew, but somehow Dale reached out and caught them in his hand!** My very own Superman.

Dale's roommate had a cousin in Roslindale, a suburb of Boston. They often went to her apartment on weekends to get away from the post. She also did their laundry sometimes and this was one of those weeks. We stopped at her apartment, and Dale went up to get their clothes while we waited in the car. Afterwards, we went out to the post, and I got to see the barracks and the post where he lived and worked. It was my first time on an Army post. Little did I know the part it would play in my future!

The weekend ended much too quickly, and too soon we were back at Logan Airport. Dale and I said our good-byes, and I was crying as I boarded a much smaller airplane from Mohawk Airlines. I watched as the plane taxied away and Dale became smaller and smaller. *Oooops! What was that lurch? Is this plane safe?* I soon realized that my two hour flight on American Airlines was more like a five and a half hour trip on Mohawk Airlines – or Slowhawk, as I named it. On this flight, we went up and down at three different airports, and my stomach lurched and churned with each landing and take-off. The stewardess kept bringing me lemonade... *it would make me feel better she said. It made things worse!* Finally, there was Detroit in the window! We were bouncing to a stop- hallelujah! My mind was made up – never again! Airplanes and I were not made for each other, and I was done with them. Once again, my future was hitting me, but I was unaware and oblivious to my future.

Back to work I went the next day and the drudgery of working in the factory. If anything, it solidified my decision to complete college. This was definitely not for me. I had never understood before what all of the people working in factories had to go through every day, but I knew I could not do it.

Dale called me late in the month. I wasn't home when he called; Bonnie and I had gone to see the movie *Cat Ballou*, and I had gotten home late. He still wanted me to call him, though, so I made the call... I wasn't ready for the conversation that followed. It seemed that the wonderful weekend in Boston wasn't as wonderful as I had thought. I listened as he talked, and my heart twisted and turned. *He had found someone new... his roommate's cousin... remember we stopped at her apartment... they were planning a future together... he was sorry... it had just happened... he hadn't planned it.* Goodbye.

It was over. Six years. My heart stopped. My anger burst out. Why? What happened? Our wedding plans... invitations, the shower, our plans. What do I tell our friends? How do I go on? *My life feels over. It feels so empty. I feel like Scarlett O'Hara...*Tomorrow, tomorrow is another day.

Bloom Where You Are Planted

Looking back on Christmas 1965, I realize the pall that was gripping my family, and yet, I realize what fun we had that year! For me, it was one of my favorite Christmases.

1965 had been a rough year. Early in the year, my dad had to declare bankruptcy, losing not only his grocery store – The Grandway Market in South Lyon, Michigan – but also our home on Shadywood Court in Plymouth. It nearly killed him, and he was very depressed. For me, I had to leave Michigan State University after the spring trimester and get a job. During the summer, Dale and I had broken our engagement, just weeks before the wedding. For all of us, it was a difficult time.

We moved into a two bedroom, one bath, two level apartment on Parkview Drive. The back of the house faced a major street, Mill Street, and across that street was a factory.

The neighborhood was "well worn" and far from Daddy's dreams. He went to work for Jim Elias as a meat cutter and then found a job at Kroger's. For a while, he worked both jobs to make ends meet. Mom went to work at Dunning's in town. It was a women's dress shop but also sold clothing for girls and young children. I found a job, first as a gift wrapper at Crowley's, a local chain department store, then at Burrough's, the adding machine company, as a file clerk. Each day, I walked through the factory and collected oily "machine spec" cards, carried them back to the office, and filed them. The factory was HOT and DIRTY. It was a time before "sexual harassment" was recognized, and the men were quite vulgar at times with their comments and cat calls. I was not happy. At home, my eight year old sister Susie and I were sharing a bedroom.

Things began to improve in August. I was laid off by Burrough's and found a much better job at St. Mary's hospital in neighboring Livonia. My job was as a switchboard operator at the main desk. Our phone system was antiquated. I wore headphones and pulled cords and plugged them back into numbered holes that represented the hospital rooms and offices. It was actually fun, and I learned a lot on that phone board. At the same time, they supported my desire to go back to school and scheduled my hours around my class schedule at Schoolcraft Community College, just a couple of miles from the hospital. I also served as a bridesmaid for my friends Rick and Mary's wedding and began a relationship with Jim, but that is another story.

As Christmas approached, our family faced a holiday with very little money in a dreary apartment that fell short of anyplace we had ever lived. The living room was hardly able to fit our furniture, let alone a Christmas tree. But we found a way to put the tree up and place all of our precious ornaments on its branches. It was our tree as it had always been, and it helped to brighten our spirits. The living room had a stairway that went to our bedrooms upstairs. We had never had a stairway before, so it afforded a new challenge in decorating for us. My crafty side came into play. I bought some inexpensive red and white felt, glue, and silver glitter. Susie and I worked together and made Christmas stockings for all of us with our names on them. We bought some inexpensive garland and draped it along the stairway, hanging the socks along the wall as well. We cut additional shapes from the left over felt and glued them on a white sheet, making a skirt for the Christmas tree. This would be the first year we had ever had stockings and a tree skirt, and we used them for many years to come.

Susie and I had never had a chance to work together before, the ten year difference in our ages was a major challenge for us. But she was now eight years old and, we were able to "glue" ourselves together as sisters. After we finished decorating, we took up Christmas baking. We made the sugar cookies, cutting them into the many shapes and decorating them with colored icing and colored sprinkles. Momma joined us to make her spiral cookies, nut balls, and her filled cookies. As we worked together in the small kitchen, we sang Christmas carols and laughed.

There weren't to be many presents under the tree, so I suggested we buy small gifts and fill each others' Christmas socks. I helped Susie make small gifts for the socks such as woven potholders for Momma. I had gotten a loan that was paying my school fees, so I used my check from the hospital to buy gifts for my family. I was able to get Daddy a footstool – the lid opened up and he could store his books and magazines inside. Momma got a new red purse, and Susie got a new doll. It made me feel good to buy these gifts for my family.

As was my father's practice, he woke me up on Christmas Eve morning and gave me some money with directions to go buy his gift for my mom! He always gave me special directions as to what I was to buy – usually perfume, or a night gown, maybe a purse or gloves. This Christmas, it was a warm bath robe for Mom. So, once we got underway, Susie and I went shopping up town to find Mom a bath robe. We only had two ladies' stores in Plymouth, Dunnings where Mom worked and Minerva's. Since Mom was working, we went to Minerva's to do our shopping. We found a pretty pink robe with lace around the collar and little flowers embroidered down the front.

As Christmas morning dawned, we all gathered in the living room around the tree. We opened our gifts and the things in our stockings. We laughed, and we shared the joy of Christmas morning. It didn't seem like we were struggling that morning. Later in the day, Uncle Kenny and Aunt Billie came over for Christmas dinner. Mom made a complete turkey dinner with Aunt Billie's help and after dinner, Daddy and Uncle Kenny fell asleep on the sofa. Jim came over and joined our family before we left for Christmas evening at his house. Jim's sister Chris was one of my best friends, and I had grown up with his family – gathering around the piano at their house to sing

Christmas carols. The perfect ending to a perfect day...

When I look back on this Christmas, I realize all that I learned that year that would carry me through many Christmas seasons in the future. Our family survived a sparse Christmas with joy and love. We had worked together in making decorations to brighten our home and spirits and in the baking of Christmas goodies. Susie and I had become closer as sisters, a closeness that would only continue to grow stronger as the years have gone by. And we realized that no matter where we lived, family and friends would always be there to add to the joy and blessings of the season.

I've been able to use these lessons throughout my life. As a military family, we have celebrated Christmas in many different homes, in many different countries, climates, and states. We have had lean years and years of plenty. The one thing that has always remained a constant, though, has been our tradition – family and friends are always the center of our celebrations, and no matter where we are, we have learned to bloom where we were planted...

Twenty-Nine Years in the Making

The day was May 22, 1993, and it had taken me twenty-nine years to get to this day. It was my graduation day, graduation from Eckerd College in St. Petersburg, Florida.

The road to this day was long and winding, but here I was at last, graduating from college. This had always been my dream, from the earliest age. People would ask me what I wanted to be when I grew up, and I would answer, "A teacher." There was never any doubt that I would go to college; my goal was Michigan State University. All through elementary school and high school, I worked hard to get the grades that would provide me with a scholarship. And lo and behold, upon graduation from Plymouth High School in June of 1964, I held in my hand my cherished scholarship to Michigan State University.

In September of 1964, we loaded up the car, and I moved to North Case Hall at Michigan State University (MSU). My best friend Bonnie was my roommate, and we shared our room with another girl, Barb. Together, we weathered those first days away from home – teaching Barb how to make a bed and do laundry, homesickness, studying harder than ever before, and being on our own. We enjoyed college football games, trips into Lansing to see movies and shop, train rides home to Plymouth for weekend visits, and the strength of our friendships. We had one other new experience that fall at MSU. Case Hall was the first integrated dorm, and we were on the one integrated floor with white girls in rooms on one side of the hall and the black girls in rooms on the other side. These were the first black girls I had ever really met, and we got along really well. The two girls across the hall from our room were dating two of the football players, and we thought that was really great – they even introduced us to them!

But, back home in my family, things were not quite as they seemed. My dad's business was failing, and he was facing bankruptcy. They were trying hard to support my college expenses, but it was becoming increasingly more difficult. My college had always been my dad's dream. He had only a ninth grade education, and no one in his family had ever gone to college. So, when his business failed and I had to withdraw from MSU after only two terms, it was not just my disappointment, it was his failure. One he would carry for twenty-nine years.

Coming home from MSU didn't mean that I quit trying. I got a job and worked so that I could go to Schoolcraft Community College while living at home. I managed to complete my second year there and then to transfer to Eastern Michigan University in the fall of 1966. Eastern Michigan University was in Ypsilanti (ip-si-lan-ti), Michigan, about sixteen miles from my home. With another of my high school friends, Chris, I rented an apartment, continued working, and kept working on a college degree. But, now I was twenty-one, and my high school sweetheart Dale, asked me to be his wife (again), an offer I could not turn down. After one semester at Eastern Michigan, I left college behind me and became a wife and eventually a mother. My dream of a college education became an unfulfilled thing of the past.

Dale and I traveled with the Army, and I received a much different education, a more hands on education. We traveled through Europe and visited the actual sites of history, and we lived within the local communities in both Germany and Italy, learning their cultures. In our movements within the United States, we were again able to learn about American history through the actual sites where it took place. But, I still did not have a college diploma.

Finally, in 1987, our family arrived in Tampa, Florida. I began working as the Program Director at Girl Scouts of Suncoast Council, not knowing that it would lead to a dream fulfilled. The first two years at Suncoast Council were uneventful other than the fact that my job was very satisfying and one I enjoyed immensely. But all of that was to change in January of 1990.

Rosemary Holliday joined our staff in January 1990. She was one of the most dynamic people I had ever encountered, and she became my supervisor. Immediately she began asking questions: *"Where do you want to be in five years?" " How do you plan to get there?" " What do you plan to do about your education?" "Have you ever thought about completing your education?"* She never gave up until she heard the answers she wanted to hear, BUT more than that, she never stopped until I wanted the same things.

And by June 1990, I found myself enrolled in classes at Eckerd College in St. Petersburg.

The program was designed for adult learners. It was named PEL – Program for Experienced Learners – and designed for adults who had been out of school for a while, held jobs, and quite possibly had families. It was an energetic program with eight week terms. Classes were held in the evening and on Saturday. We did the same work expected of students taking full semesters in the regular college program. But the highlight of the program was our ability to write essays about our life experiences and use those experiences for college credits. The experiential essays had to be in great detail and had to be verified by supervisors and those who could speak for the subject. This meant tracking down former supervisors and people from my past. In this way, I was able to "comp" the maximum five courses including my internship in a non-profit organization – the Girl Scouts.

Now, on May 22, 1993, with my Mom and Dad, my husband and two of my children in the audience, I was fulfilling my dream. My Dad was on the verge of drifting away into dementia – all day long he thought this was my wedding day! But, when I donned my cap and gown, he realized I was graduating from college. All of the hard work was more than worthwhile when I saw the look on my Dad's face. He and I had finally fulfilled the dream – I had the diploma he had always wanted for me, and I had the education I had dreamed of since childhood. It only took twenty-nine years.......

The Motorcycle on My Hand

The summer of 1964 was a busy time. Dale and I had graduated from Plymouth High School in June and started making plans for the rest of our lives. First on the agenda was getting ready for college in the fall. Dale was working at a gas station near our house, and I was working as a cashier for my dad in South Lyon, Michigan. The idea was to save money for school, or so I thought.

When September arrived, I packed up my life and moved to Michigan State University in East Lansing, Michigan. Dale remained in Plymouth and started classes at Schoolcraft Community College in nearby Livonia, Michigan. Well, Dale decided he needed transportation and used his wages to buy a Honda motorcycle. He loved that bike, and I learned to ride on the seat behind him – but it scared me to death. Dale made the most of it with a black jacket and all the trimmings of a bike rider.

Christmas break arrived, and I came home for the holidays. Dale and I began thinking about getting married earlier than planned, and we went shopping for engagement rings. I fell in love with a solitaire diamond, and we put it on layaway to hold it. Between Christmas and New Year's Eve, we were invited to the engagement party of our friends Mary and Rick. Only thing was, Dale never showed up! Even his parents didn't know where he was! He did show up the next morning, however, with a major, life changing announcement – he had enlisted in the Army! Ten days later, we bid him farewell at the Detroit Induction Center, and our lives began to change.

I returned to Michigan State with every intention of completing my college education while living for the mail every day. Letters from Dale were few and far between, but the day finally came when he completed basic training and came home on leave. I took the train from Lansing to Plymouth so that I could be there to meet him when he flew home. His dad and I dared the elements and a snow storm to go to the airport to meet him, but it was a glorious homecoming, and I was sooo happy to see him again. We saw each other through the weekend, and then I returned to school, only to return home the next weekend as well.

Dale and I went out that Saturday night and, to my surprise, he had my engagement ring! He made it official and asked me to marry him. I was in heaven! And I had a shiny, sparkly ring on my left hand. I didn't think to ask him how he had gotten it off layaway, I just enjoyed watching it sparkle. I soon learned, though, how the magic had happened. He had sold his motorcycle to pay off my ring – a fact that I would be reminded of for the next fifty plus years!

Many years have passed since then, and my ring has managed to continue having a story all of its own. It seems that Dale and I decided not to get married a few months after these exciting days. Instead, we decided to go our separate ways. He was stationed in Massachusetts at the time, and we broke up by telephone! I didn't want to keep the ring, so I put it in its box and took it over to Dale's mother. That was August of 1965, and I hoped I would never see him ever again!

We were both dating other people, and I had even changed schools. I was now living on my own in an apartment and attending Eastern Michigan University in Ypsilanti, Michigan. In the meantime, Dale had finished school in Massachusetts and was stationed in Germany. Our lives were going along quite nicely, I thought. Until June, when I received a card from Dale and then a telephone call. We talked, but only as friends – his life wasn't going as well as he had planned. The calls continued through the summer, and in September 1966, he asked the fateful question once more.

Needless to say, the ring came out of storage – his mom's safe deposit box – and went back on my left hand. It was as shiny as I remembered, and it was now back where it belonged. And on February 11, 1967, it was joined by its accompanying wedding band. I thought the ring would never leave my hand again.

Wrong. One afternoon during the summer of 1985, as I was walking to my car, my two teenage sons decided to be funny and throw a basketball at me. In making an attempt to avoid the ball, I raised my hands and in so doing, jammed the three fingers on my left hand. They swelled so quickly I could not remove my rings – the hospital had to cut them off. I was devastated. My rings were very important to me. The jeweler told us that the rings were too damaged to be fixed. We moved the diamond to a new setting, but I never wore it; it languished in a jewelry box beside the original setting.

Twenty-six years passed without me wearing my rings. But Christmas morning 2011 arrived, and I was to receive a very special gift. It seems my daughter, Julie, had found a jeweler who felt he could fix my original setting, and fix it he did. He reset the diamond, managing to preserve the original inscription, and made the bands whole again. And now, fifty-two years after first placing the ring on my finger, it is back in its place, and we can once again admire the motorcycle on my hand!

No More Bridges!!

The summer of 1966 found my life changing rapidly. I had been accepted to Eastern Michigan University for the fall semester. The university was about sixteen miles from Plymouth in Ypsilanti, Michigan. My friend Chris Cutler and I rented a two-bedroom apartment in Ypsi (Ypsilanti). At long last, I was truly living on my own. Chris and I would be living in the apartment during the summer and in September, we would be joined by two more roommates, Ruth and Suzie.

Our apartment complex was brand new and our apartment very modern. When you walked into our apartment, you walked into the living/dining room area. There was a long bar that separated the kitchen from the dining room. Chris and I shared the very large master bedroom with a walk-in closet. Suzie and Ruth would be sharing the smaller room but it was much larger than a dorm room!

Daddy gave me his 1964 Ford Falcon so that I could get to my job at Hawthorn Center in Livonia and back to school in Ypsi. It was also handy to get to classes at Eastern since our apartment was about ten blocks from campus and the nearest grocery store was about a mile away. Among the four of us, it was the only car!

About six weeks before moving into the apartment I had fallen and broken my leg while out bowling with friends from work. Now, everyone will tell you that I was drunk at the time BUT, I wasn't twenty-one yet so I couldn't get drinks at the bowling alley, only pop. However, I did live up to my nickname, Miss Grace. The break was just above my knee and hard to cast. So, the doctor used two pieces of hard plastic taped together to stabilize the break. It was terribly uncomfortable! I was also on crutches, making the stairs at my parent's house really hard to navigate. My sister was trying to help down the stairs one morning, going ahead of me, when I lost my balance! We almost went down the stairs together, in a heap! We didn't try that again. The break had healed by the time I moved into the apartment.

Chris and I decided to take a camping trip that summer. Our parents agreed as long as we stayed in the state of Michigan. We decided to go to the Upper Peninsula and to leave on July 5th. Using our well learned Girl Scout camping skills, we planned our meals and gathered the necessary utensils we would need for cooking. Chris' dad had an old Army tent that we had used in her back yard during high school summers. We made our bedrolls, packed our clothes and headed out. Chris and I had always been tent-mates on Girl Scout camping trips making us confident of our camping skills.

We left early on the morning of July 5th, headed north. My little Falcon was packed to the gills with all of our gear. The temperature was warm, in the mid-80's. All was well until we hit the tree line about half-way up the state. That's when my allergy kicked in and I started sneezing and my eyes started itching! It was just like all of our trips to Interlochen in high school, BUT, this time I was ready! We stopped and I took an allergy pill. No more sneezing!

We made it to Mackinaw in late afternoon and decided to cross the bridge and camp for the night in the Upper Peninsula. We had no idea that would be an adventure! I was driving as we started across the Mackinaw Bridge, a free-standing bridge. As we crossed, the wind picked up and the bridge began to sway slightly. Well, that afternoon, the wind was extremely high and I began to have trouble keeping the car in its lane. We would drift into the next lane and back again! Now you all know the reason I am afraid of crossing bridges! I made a decision that we would be going home through Wisconsin! I was not going over that bridge ever again! Besides our own adventure, a car sometime after our car, was blown off the bridge and into the Straits. They closed the bridge for the first time in its history!

The strong winds continued once we were off the bridge. We were tired and hungry, so we pulled into the first campgrounds off the bridge. The campground sat on soft white sand, presenting us with our first challenge. With the strong winds blowing and the soft sand, there was no way that our tent pegs were going to stay anchored in the ground. We couldn't pitch the tent, so we repacked the car and drove further down the road to a campground that was not on the beach. We were able to pitch the tent and set up camp.

Our next challenge was the weather. We had packed clothes that were appropriate for the warm temperatures in the lower peninsula. But, when the sun went down in the Upper Peninsula, the temperatures dropped into the 30's and low 40's! We ate a quick supper, put on extra clothes and climbed into our sleeping bags by seven o'clock! We still froze but it was warmer in our sleeping bags and we fell asleep for the night.

Early to bed and early to rise... We were up bright and early the next morning and ready to explore. After a quick breakfast of cold cereal, we packed up our campsite and drove to Tahquamenon Falls where we found a beautiful place to pitch our tent. The next day we hiked into the falls. I would probably consider this hike and the falls to be one of the top experiences in my life. This is the area where Longfellow took inspiration to write the *Song of Hiawatha*. The falls themselves were beautiful, the unspoiled natural setting only added to their beauty.

Our trip continued with a stop at Sault Ste. Marie where we watched a ship go through from the lower Great Lakes to Lake Superior. From Sault Ste. Marie we traveled to Mackinac Island. We spent a day wandering around the island visiting the old fort and the Grand Hotel. There were beautiful views everywhere we stopped on the island. Of course, the high point of the trip was our stop at the candy shop where we bought our share of Mackinac Island fudge.

It was time to go home and I still felt the safest way was to go home through Wisconsin – no bridges to cross! Instead, Chris drove the car and I sat on the floor of the car as we once again crossed the Mackinaw Bridge. I will forever appreciate the beauty of the bridge as I admire it from the shore. Many years later I felt the same way about the beauty of the Sunshine Skyway in St. Petersburg, Florida, but that's another story for another day.

Back home again, we welcomed our roommates Suzie and Ruth. Set up caper charts for our duties in the apartment, registered for our classes and settled in for another school year. A school year that would change my life forever.

Coming Back Together

1966 was a busy year. First, I broke my leg bowling with friends from work. Being laid up gave me lots of time to study and when our grades came out in May, I was on the dean's list. Somehow, Mrs. Cunningham, Dale's mom, found out about all of that and told Dale in one of his letters. The next thing I knew, I received a get well card and letter from him. And that was the beginning....

All through the summer, while I moved into the apartment, camped in the Upper Peninsula, and worked at my job, Dale and I were writing letters to each other. The letters were friendly and full of general chitchat. Meanwhile, there was a war raging in Southeast Asia – Viet Nam.

In early September, I received **THE LETTER,** the one that was to change my life. Dale asked me to marry him once again. The decision on my part was not automatic and did not come easy. The letter was followed by a phone call from Dale in Germany to me in the states. He pled his case to me – he was lonely, he missed me, he didn't like living in the barracks, he realized how much he loved me. He wanted me to join him in Germany. I needed time.

I went home and talked to my mother and to my dad. My mom listened and asked questions – what about school and my degree? What about the last time when he broke the engagement, how did I feel about that and did I trust him? Germany was a long way away, was I ready to make that commitment? Daddy took a different stand. If Dale ever stepped back in our house again he would kill him!! If I decided to marry him, he wouldn't walk me down the aisle! Even my friends took different stands. Chris was all for it. After all, she had been with us through all of our high school ups and downs and she felt we were supposed to be together. Bonnie was not happy about it at all. She did not like Dale and had been with me the night Dale broke our first engagement. What was I going to do?

Well, my heart won out over my head. I called him back in Germany and accepted his proposal. The plans started immediately. First was my ring. It was still at his parent's house, so I was to go over and get the ring from his mom. She wasn't real happy either but she gave me my ring back and I began to become part of the Cunningham family.

Now, I was already into the new school year and I still had my job. Within a month, we had a wedding date – February 11, 1967, four short months away. My mind whirled with all the plans I needed to make – there were church plans to make, dresses to pick for my wedding party, a cake to select, I needed a passport, and on and on and on…...

The first big change came at work. I had been working in the locked ward at Hawthorn Center. But Hawthorn Center had taken over a building at Northville State Hospital, the children's ward. The children here had been hospitalized for a very long time and were more difficult. I was transferred to the new unit and I was transferred to night shift. Neither fact made me happy. All the doors in the new unit were locked and the patients were very strong and had been socialized to their way of life there. They realized I was new to this environment and they took advantage of that, challenging me at every turn. At Thanksgiving time, the final straw was broken. One of the girls on the ward managed to block me into the laundry room. She was very threatening, telling me, "I am going to kill you," and she had the size and anger to accomplish it. One of the male attendants heard her and got the help of two other male attendants and they came to my rescue. That was the end. I turned in my two weeks notice and gave a sigh of relief.

In the meantime, I was still taking classes and really getting into the excitement of my wedding. Chris and my friend Mary were going to serve as my senior attendants and my sister Susie was going to be my junior attendant. We went shopping together and we found a beautiful dress that all could wear. Susie's had to be made to match. The dresses were pink and their headpiece was a halo ring with a small veil. We got their shoes died to match, while I found white satin shoes to wear. I already had my dress but now I had to have it fitted and I had to select a veil. The veil I chose was a crown of pearls and lace with a fingertip veil.

Winter break came for school and I now had to move home to my parents. My "room" would be the basement for the short two months I would live there, it was hard leaving my apartment, it had been my first adult home.

Dale's mom was planning a shower for me but also giving me problems. She was refusing to get a dress for the wedding. She and I came to a standstill over the dress and I told her, "If you wear a black dress to my wedding, I will carry you down the aisle and drop you in a snow pile!" I was furious. Well, I called Dale in Germany and told him he needed to find the solution. He called his dad and gave the problem to him. Dad Cunningham was always crafty about getting around Mom. He called her best friend and arranged a shopping trip, giving the money to her friend to buy a new dress. It worked! Mom Cunningham selected a seafoam green brocade suit that looked wonderful on her.

My mom and I stayed busy with all the little details of the wedding. We sent out the invitations, selected the cake and flowers, planned the decorations for the reception at the church. As a child, she would always take me to downtown Detroit to get a new dress for school. So, we took one last shopping trip to downtown Detroit and J. L. Hudson's. I picked out two new dresses, a suit to travel in, and a new coat. There were also new shoes and some slacks and tops. It was a wonderful day and we closed it out with our traditional trip to

Sanders candy shop for a hot fudge sundae. We had so much fun!

January that year was very cold and snowy and it was my last month of school. Eastern Michigan crews tried hard to keep all of the walkways on campus clear but it wasn't always easy. One day, as I was leaving my psychology class, my mind far away, I slid down a full set of icy steps on my back! I quickly got up and brushed myself off and walked four blocks to my car, denying that I was in pain! Now, I could drive ten blocks to my apartment or I could drive fourteen miles home to my parents' house. I'm not sure why, but I chose to drive home to Plymouth. My back and my neck grew stiffer with each mile and I had a hard time finding the brakes. But, I managed to get home, out of the car and in the back door of the house where I passed out. My dad found me when he got home from work and got me into bed. Two weeks before my wedding and the week before final exams at school. We had to reschedule my exams for February – after the wedding and before we left for Germany!

Dale arrived home one week before the wedding. A snow storm had been predicted and we were afraid he wouldn't get in. It was snowing when he landed but the blizzard waited one more day! He went straight from the airport to Lents Men's Wear in Plymouth to be fitted for his tux. On Saturday night, we went to a party given for us at my apartment, we both drank just a little too much! My dad was at work during the blizzard so Dale shoveled the snow for him. We received three feet of snow!

My twenty-first birthday was on Wednesday and we had dinner with my parents at home. I had promised my dad that I wouldn't get married until I turned twenty-one and I was keeping my promise by three days.

Now, it was time. Our wedding day had arrived. We had overcome so many obstacles along the way, but that was over. It was time....

I Do

February 11, 1967, dawned icy cold and clear. The three feet of snow glistened in the bright sun, and my breath could be seen as I left the house for Althea's beauty shop. Today was my day, my very special wedding day. I could not believe that it was finally here.

Last night, I spent my last night in my parent's house as Sandy Fielden. Following our rehearsal dinner, we had returned home – just the four of us, Mom, Dad, Susie and me. It seemed like no one wanted to go to bed, and we sat in the basement and talked and laughed about our family. I sat on Daddy's lap and cried as I faced a new life with joy and fear mixed together.

I didn't sleep well that night and woke early. Woke to that beautiful morning. Mom, Susie and I left for Althea's while Daddy stayed home and washed and waxed the car to its shiny best. When we returned from Althea's, our wedding party was at the house decorating the cars that would take us to the church that night and then on our honeymoon. I kept wanting to pinch myself, *"Was today really here? Were Dale and I finally getting married after all these years?"*

About noon, Auntie Arvella and Uncle Harry arrived so that Auntie Arvella could help Mom with all the last minute details. We listened to the latest weather report and feared the worst as more snow was forecast. That meant my aunt and cousins from Grand Rapids wouldn't be able to come. Soon Uncle Kenny and Aunt Billie arrived from Detroit with Uncle Kenny's booming "Where's the bride hiding?" They, too, had arrived to help Mom and Dad get ready.

Meanwhile, in the back of the house, my little sister, Susan, who was ten years old at the time, was keeping me quite busy. I was trying to pack for my honeymoon, and she was determined to play hi-jinks on me! Every time I turned my back, she would throw a handful of rice in my suitcase! She was very determined!

Mom and Auntie Arvella were busy pressing our dresses one last time when Aunt Delores, Marie, and Don and Lil arrived from Grand Rapids! That was a surprise because it was snowing in Plymouth. Our small house was filling up with early arrivals for the wedding! We were fast reaching standing room only in the living room. Auntie Arvella pressed my veil and hung it over a lamp shade to help keep its shape. All of my uncles smoked so it really wasn't a surprise that there was a small burn spot in my veil when I put it on that night.

Soon it was 6:00 PM and time for the wedding party to leave for the church. My aunts, uncles, and cousins would follow later. We drove to the church as my stomach churned away. *"This is really happening. I am really on my way to the church to marry Dale."* We arrived at the church, and Dad parked the car at the side of the church and, carrying our dresses and head pieces, we walked into the church. We went to the parlor next to the sanctuary where we were to get dressed. Dale and the men were getting dressed downstairs.

Mary and Chris arrived, my two senior attendants. Susie was my junior attendant. Mary did not look too well, she was really pale, and, suddenly, she ran out the front door of the church and threw up in the bushes! That was how we learned that she was pregnant! With that excitement over, we all proceeded to get dressed. Gertie Thorpe, a good friend of our family, helped us get dresses, hats, and flowers all assembled. And suddenly, it was 7:00 PM.

However, nothing was happening. Nothing except that the church ushers kept coming into the parlor to get chairs. Then, Reverend Williams came through the basement and up into our room to ask why we weren't getting started. An usher came in at that time and told us that people were still arriving and that there was standing room only in the sanctuary! With snow falling outside, our friends and family had come to our wedding.

Soon Margaret began to sing "Oh, Promise Me," and then the organist began the wedding march. I held my breath; it was time. I entered the back of the sanctuary on my dad's arm and, for the first time, saw the beauty of the church bathed in candlelight. With friends and family lining the aisles and across the back of the church, Daddy and I walked down the aisle. At the front of the church stood Dale, tall and straight and smiling at me.

As Daddy and I reached the front of the church, he gave me a kiss and placed my hand in Dale's. There was a hush in the church as Dale and I repeated our vows and then lit one single candle from our individual candles. Reverend Williams said a prayer and then pronounced the words I had waited a lifetime to hear, "I now pronounce you husband and wife." Dale gave me a kiss and then we turned to face our family and friends; "Let me introduce you to Mr.

and Mrs. Cunningham," I heard the minister say. Then everyone stood up and applauded as we walked back up the aisle.

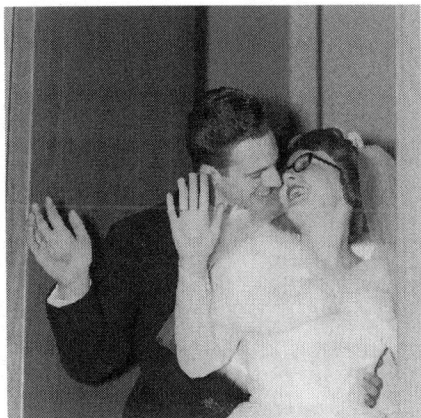

My heart was beating fast and the smile on my face must have reached from ear to ear! After eight years of dating, fighting, and dating again, we were married. Our reception was held in the church basement where we did all the traditional things. We cut our cake, I threw my bouquet, we greeted our guests, and then, it was time to leave. Time to begin our new life together as Mr. and Mrs. Cuningham.

That was fifty years ago. Every minute is still crystal clear in my mind and my memories. We have lived so much life since that day – three children, Kenny, Jason, and Julie; nine beautiful grandchildren – Allura, Tim, Briana, Addison, Jason Jr., Nathan, Amber, SamBob, and Wesley; and most recently Evelyn, our great-granddaughter. We've laughed and cried, celebrated and mourned, held each other up through illness, and thanked the Lord for the richness of our lives. Yes, fifty years ago I spoke two little words that have held my life together since: "I do," and I will until the day the Lord calls me home.

You Can't Go Home Again... Oh, Wait!

I recently went back to that small town, Plymouth, Michigan. It has made some changes since I was a child growing up there. The biggest change, it's no longer a small town surrounded by farms. It's now a very cosmopolitan suburb of Detroit. What once were farms, are now very posh subdivisions and Plymouth is "the place to be!"

Kellogg Park is still in the center of town. They still hold band concerts there every Friday night during the summer, a custom started while I was in high school by Mr. Griffith. People come from all around to hear these concerts, lining their chairs and blankets up early in the day to get the very best spots. What once were small shops, Kresge's, Lent's Men's Clothing store, The Small Professor Book Shop and so on, are now small cafés and restaurants. The National Bank of Detroit is a Greek restaurant! Patrons sit at quaint little tables along the sidewalks and watch others pass by. The old Box Bar, a town staple all of my life, has been sold and will soon be an Italian restaurant. We had lunch there one last time for old times sake.

Many of the old buildings are gone or have been repurposed. The Masonic Temple building on the corner by the park is gone and, in its place is a new office building with apartments on the top floor. The Mayflower Hotel has been torn down and a new building with businesses on the street level and apartments on the upper two levels. When we were in school, the hotel was owned by the father of one of our classmates. The Wilcox house has been restored and stands proudly at the top of the park. The Wilcox family was one of the founding families in Plymouth.

Plymouth High School, where I attended high school, is still standing but now is run by Plymouth Parks and Recreation. Adult education classes are held in the classrooms as well as craft courses. The gym allows for youth and adult sports activities while the pool is open to the public for lessons and open swims. The main auditorium is utilized by the Plymouth Theater Guild for local plays. In the small park located in front of the school, you'll now find the "Plymouth Rock", moved here from Kellogg Park. The old canon has also been moved here. And, as a reminder to our generation, the Viet Nam Memorial has been placed here as well with the names of classmates who served in that war but never came home. My friend Chris Cutler's house, where I had lunch all through high school, which stood two houses from the school, is now gone and another large office building stands in its place. Bode's restaurant by the train tracks is still there and I am told it still offers a mean bowl of chili.

I visited each of the houses I lived in while growing up. 744 South Harvey is still there. But the street is changing. Many of the small houses originally on South Harvey have been torn down and "mini-mansions" have taken their place. I can't help but wonder how long our little house will remain there. 799 Pacific is also still standing and occupied. Where it once had asbestos shingle siding, it now has modern aluminum siding. The backyard is enclosed by a tall, wooden privacy fence. But the blue spruce tree that I helped Daddy plant when I was eight years old is still there, now grown taller than the house. I wish Daddy could see it, he was so proud of that tree. Our house on Shadywood Court in Lake Pointe Village is also still there. However, the street has changed. The house next door, once owned by Curly Gray is gone, taken down to allow for the building of interstate 275 behind our street. Our house has added a two car garage but otherwise, it really hasn't changed all that much. Our house at 797 North Harvey has acquired new aluminum siding with new landscaping. The big maple tree out front is gone but otherwise, it remains pretty much as we knew it.

Dale grew up on Ball Street in what was then nicknamed Muddy

Meadows. The once "muddy" streets are all paved now. The house he grew up in now has aluminum siding, a picket fence in the back yard. The lot behind the house where they grew vegetables, including his dreaded asparagus which he mowed down, is now occupied by a new house.

Yes, Plymouth has changed in the past many years I have been gone. But it is still my home town and I still feel very much part of it. Going "home" still soothes my soul and renews my inner spirit. I will always be a Plymothite.

About the Author

Sandy Cunningham lives in Florida with her husband of 51 years. They are a retired military family, having lived several years in Europe. Their three children, nine grandchildren and first great-grandchild all live nearby. Retired from her own career in a non-profit service organization, Sandy teaches Life Writing courses to other senior citizens through the local library system while working on the stories of her own life. She stays busy with her family, writing, genealogy and cross-stitching.

Made in the USA
San Bernardino, CA
09 March 2018